EXPLORING THE
SPANISH ARMADA

WINIFRED GLOVER is curator of Ethnography in the Department of Archaeology and Ethnography in the Ulster Museum in Belfast. A graduate of Queen's University, Belfast, her special interests include the history of ethnographic collections and the Armada collection. She has published widely in archaeological and historical journals and has written catalogues of the Ulster Museum's collections.

EXPLORING

the **Spanish Armada**

Winifred Glover

THE O'BRIEN PRESS
DUBLIN

In association with National Museums and Galleries
of Northern Ireland, Ulster Museum, Belfast

First published in hardback 2000 by The O'Brien Press Ltd,
20 Victoria Road, Dublin 6, Ireland.
Tel. +353 1 4923333; Fax. +353 1 4922777
E-mail books@obrien.ie
Website www.obrien.ie

ISBN 0-86278-646-0

British Library Cataloguing-in-Publication Data
A catalogue record for this title is available
from the British Library

1 2 3 4 5 6 7 8 9
00 01 02 03 04 05 06

The O'Brien Press receives
assistance from

The Arts Council
An Chomhairle Ealaíon

Editing, typesetting, layout and design: The O'Brien Press Ltd
Illustrations: Deirdre Crone
Maps: Deirdre Crone
Colour separations: C&A Print Services Ltd
Printing: Biddles Ltd

For my family

ACKNOWLEDGEMENTS

The author and publisher would like to thank the Trustees and Chief Executive of the Museums and Galleries of Northern Ireland for their permission to publish the Ulster Museum's Armada collection; the publishers Anthony Nelson for permission to include extracts from 'The Spanish Armada Wrecks of Ireland' in *Excavating Ships of War, Vol. II*; the National Maritime Museum, London, for permission to reproduce 'Hellburners of Antwerp'; Alan Carey, private collection, for permission to reproduce 'The Wrecking of a Spanish Galleon off Port na Spaniagh'; Penguin Putnam Inc. for permission to reproduce one photograph and text from *Treasures of the Armada* by Robert Sténuit. The author acknowledges references taken from the Calendar of State Papers (Ireland), 1588–1605, and the Calendar of Letters and State Papers relating to English Affairs, preserved in Simancas, Vol. IV, 1587–1603.

Many people have contributed their talents to the production of this book, chiefly Mrs Deirdre Crone of the Department of Archaeology and Ethnography, Ulster Museum, for all the drawings. The excellent photographs are the work of Bill Anderson-Porter, Michael McKeown and Bryan Rutledge of the Photographic Department, Ulster Museum. Other colleagues: Patricia McLean; Robert Heslip, Numismatics; Vivienne Pollock and Trevor Parkhill, History; Richard Warner, Cormac Bourke and Jackie Hagan, Archaeology and Ethnography, have been generous in their assistance. Thanks are due to Laurence Flanagan, retired Keeper of Antiquities of the Ulster Museum, for his enthusiasm and dedication in ensuring that the Museum acquired the collections excavated from the *Girona, La Trinidad Valencera* and the *Santa Maria de la Rosa* and in bringing the Armada collection to worldwide attention through his publications. Finally, I would like to thank Rachel Pierce of The O'Brien Press for her invaluable advice and assistance, and my family for their constant support.

CONTENTS

Introduction

I stopped in a cleft in the rock and moved three stones to
stir up the sand – still nothing. My depth gauge needle
had moved up from 30 to 20 ft. Suddenly a cliff barred my
way. Where was I! It must be the east face of Lacada Point.
The cliff ran along the edge of a vast platform leading to an
enormous rock. A white shape caught my eye. Ah! I went
closer. A lead ingot.

These words by Robert Sténuit, upon finding the first traces
of the wreck of the Spanish Armada galleass *Girona* in June
1967, heralded the culmination of years of research and the
fulfilment of a dream. The finding of a wreck-site of an
Armada ship, almost 400 years after it had sunk, would gal-
vanise the interest of the world in one of the most remarkable
historical events of all time, and would spur others on to
emulate Sténuit's dedication and success.

The story of the Spanish Armada of 1588 has fascinated
successive generations. An epic tale of ambition, loyalty,
bravery, greed and treachery, it has inspired emotions which
have resonated across the centuries. The ambition of the
Armada was breathtaking – no less so were the odds stacked
against it. What led Philip II of Spain, at the age of sixty and in
poor health, to send 130 ships of many sizes and types and
29,453 Spanish men on a hazardous journey across dangerous, uncharted waters into enemy territory? It had taken him

twenty years to finally come to the decision of invading England, so he must have felt that he had many good reasons for doing so. Why did this mighty Armada flee in disarray from what should have been the most glorious victory in the history of the Spanish Empire? And if the aim of the Armada had been the invasion of England, why have so many important sixteenth-century Spanish objects been recovered in the waters off the coast of Ireland? The answers lie in the unsteady balance of power in Europe in the sixteenth century, in the course of an epic battle and in an examination of the objects themselves, which are owned by the Ulster Museum and are on permanent display there.

This motto for the Armada is a detail from an engraving by John Pine.
It translates as *Give glory only unto your name.*

PART ONE

Preparing for Invasion

EUROPE IN THE SIXTEENTH CENTURY

Philip II inherited the Spanish throne at the age of twenty-eight from his father, Charles V, who abdicated in his favour in 1556. Charles had been a ruthless, dashing and successful king, and his boundless energy and ambition had resulted in Spain's large and far-flung empire. But the phenomenal cost of keeping hold of all his conquests began to weary him and he gratefully relinquished the monetary problems to his son, Philip, who was much more cautious and devout. Throughout his long reign, Philip agonised about the costs and difficulties of keeping the empire intact and protecting its profitable maritime trade routes from raids by English and French 'sea dogs' or pirates. In fact, the acquisition of money, either in terms of actual gold or in commanding and protecting lucrative trade routes, was at the very heart of all European conflict in the sixteenth century.

Portrait of Philip II, King of Spain, from an engraving by John Pine. He was sixty-one years old at the time of the Armada.

In 1588 it seemed as if Spain controlled half the world. As well as her own conquests in the Americas, her conquest of Portugal in 1580 and control over large parts of Holland also gave her command of their trading stations. Thus the Spanish Empire was the single largest colonising force in Europe at that time. In contrast, Queen Elizabeth did not have an empire at the time of the Spanish Armada; she did not even have control over Scotland. England was a poor country in comparison to Spain.

But for the Spanish, defending and maintaining such a vast empire had many drawbacks. It had to be protected against the Ottoman Turks on the eastern and Mediterranean sides; against France on the west; and there were rebellions in the Netherlands and in the German principalities. As Philip was to find out, in an empire's strength lies its weakness: the larger the territory to be controlled, the more vulnerable is the coloniser to attacks and rebellions by those he wishes to control.

> **GOLD**
>
> The acquisition of gold was uppermost in most traveller's minds during the centuries of exploration and discovery. In the fifteenth century, Christopher Columbus said:
>
> *Gold is the most exquisite of all things ... Whoever possesses gold can acquire all that he desires in this world. Truly, for gold he can gain entrance for his soul into paradise.*

THE REASONS FOR THE SPANISH ARMADA

Philip was a very religious man and he saw a large part of his problem in terms of religious conflict. It was during his reign that the dreaded Spanish Inquisition was set up to root out heresy in Spain and in all her colonies.

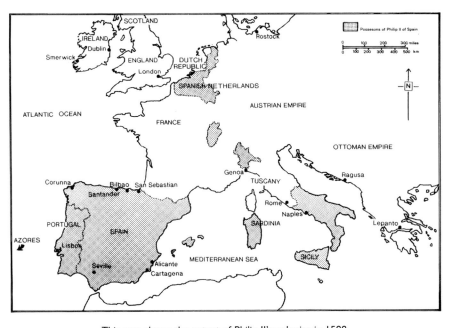

This map shows the extent of Philip II's colonies in 1588.
The Spanish Empire included: Portugal, Majorca and Menorca, Gibraltar, the Canary Islands,
East and West Indies, Mexico, Peru, Brazil, the Azores, Cape Verde Islands, the Moluccas,
the Philippines, Brabant, Luxembourg, a large part of Holland, Friesland and the island of Macao.
Spain also controlled trading stations in Guinea, Angola and Mozambique.

On his father's advice, Philip had married Mary Tudor
during the years 1554–1556, so making him king of both
Spain and England. Mary's father, Henry VIII, had divorced
her mother, Catherine of Aragon, and by doing so had
broken with Rome and begun the Reformation in England.
He had also offended Charles V, father of Philip II, because
Catherine of Aragon was his aunt. Henry's second wife,
Anne Boleyn, was not recognised by Rome, therefore his
daughter, Elizabeth, Mary's half-sister, was regarded as illegitimate. Mary was a devout Catholic and during her short
reign she attempted to reimpose Catholicism on England by

burning 300 Protestants. These actions earned her the name 'Bloody Mary', and increased the country's hatred of the papacy. It also increased the country's hatred and suspicion of foreigners, so that they feared Spain's influence on England.

When Mary died of ill health in 1556, Philip felt he had a strong claim to the English throne because Mary had signed secret papers bequeathing the throne to her husband. For the English, however, there was no question of this happening and it was Elizabeth, not Philip, who was instated as monarch.

Portrait of Elizabeth I, Queen of England, from an engraving by John Pine. She was fifty-five years old at the time of the Armada.

Elizabeth came to the throne amid much controversy. In the eyes of the Catholic Church she was illegitimate, and because she had no heir there was also a very real danger of a struggle for succession to the throne. Both France and Spain had vested interests in putting forward their candidates. The French promoted Mary Stuart, Queen of Scots, because she was the widow of Francis I of France and she was a Catholic. Also, she was the daughter of James IV of Scotland and Henry VIII's sister, Margaret. Scotland at this time was a separate country from England and a hostile power, so a victory for Mary would mean a victory for Scotland over England. The Spanish, on the other hand, favoured Elizabeth because they wanted to have control over England, which was why Philip II offered to marry her – neatly ensuring that he would retain the crowns of Spain and England. However, Elizabeth didn't accept his offer and instead kept up a waiting game for her own clever purposes.

Spain was a very wealthy country; England was a poor country. During the 1560s, Elizabeth encouraged her sea captains, such as Francis Drake and John Hawkins, to attack and plunder Spanish colonies in the Caribbean and the Spanish treasure fleets travelling from the Americas to Seville; the trading routes were the site of the struggle for power. At the same time, Elizabeth assured the Spanish ambassador to the English court of her friendly intentions and of her promise to consider Philip's generous offer of marriage. It has to be said that Elizabeth was one of the wiliest tacticians of her time.

Relations between the two countries deteriorated for many reasons. Firstly, it was known that English Catholics were plotting to replace the Protestant Elizabeth with the Catholic Mary Stuart, as soon as Mary returned to Scotland from France after the death of her husband, Francis I. The English government believed, with good reason, that Spain backed these plots. Secondly, in 1579, the Spanish attempted to start an uprising in Ireland against the English authorities there. They joined forces with Irish exiles who had been in Europe and who had the backing of the Pope. In response to the exiles' request for assistance, the Spanish landed a force of 800 Italian and Spanish volunteers at Smerwick in County Kerry, on the western tip of Ireland. It was believed that the native Irish would join the invaders and oust the English, but this did not happen. The outcome was that both England and Spain were paranoid about the intentions of the other, and each had a network of spies to report back to their respective sovereigns.

Against this complex background of European intrigue and power play, several events took place which led directly to Philip's decision to launch an invasion force against England. In 1585–1587, Elizabeth had promoted the interests of the Pretender to the Portuguese throne, Dom Antonio, against the Spanish Crown. In the Netherlands, Protestant rebels under William of Orange had achieved many successes against the Spanish occupiers, but these came to an end with the assassination of William in 1584 – by the Spanish. In 1585, Elizabeth sent an army under her personal court favourite, Robert Dudley, Earl of Leicester, to help the Protestant rebels in Holland after the loss of their leader. In 1586, Francis Drake looted the Spanish city of Cartagena in Colombia and sacked Santo Domingo, again proving his ability to strike at wealthy Spanish colonies. In 1587, Elizabeth signed the death warrant of Mary, Queen of Scots, who was publicly beheaded at Fotheringhay Hall in Northamptonshire. Finally, Elizabeth's advocacy of Protestantism greatly irritated Pope Sixtus V, and he brought great pressure to bear on the devout Catholic King Philip to attack England and convert its people to Catholicism. Sixtus V made great efforts throughout his papacy to halt the spread of Protestantism, especially in France where intermittent wars between Protestant Huguenots and Catholics raged from 1562 to 1598. As a result of Sixtus's involvement, Philip felt that defeating England was his duty to Spain and to God – thus the obvious problems of the enterprise became obscured by the fervour of dutiful devotion.

POPE SIXTUS V

Sixtus V (1520–1590) was a Franciscan friar who progressed through the Church to become Inquisitor General in Venice, where he ruled with ruthless authority. During his term as Pope (1585–1590), his achievements were many. He oversaw the completion of St Peter's Dome in Rome and the rebuilding of the Vatican, and supervised many improvements to the city. He is chiefly famous for reforming the central administration of the Church; his model remained largely unchanged until 1962. He is also remembered as an implacable and dangerous enemy of Protestantism.

THE ARMADA OF 1588

The idea of invading England with a vast armada of ships had first been planted in Philip's mind by Don Alvaro de Bazan, Marquis of Santa Cruz, his veteran naval commander. Santa Cruz had taken Spain to victory against the Portuguese in July 1583 at the great sea battle of Terceira, one of the islands in the Azores. Strategically placed in mid-Atlantic, these islands were the last undefeated part of the Portuguese Empire. By defeating a combined Portuguese and French force there, Santa Cruz gave Spain control over all the Portuguese colonies in the Pacific and Atlantic, as well as control over the profitable Portuguese trading routes. In the light of this victory, Santa Cruz persuaded Philip that by sending a large naval fleet and army against England, victory could be his, and that the Spanish Empire could at last be free from the damage being inflicted by the English sea dogs.

The acquisition and organisation of an enormous fleet was a formidable task. Before the defeat of the Portuguese, Spain did not have a significant naval force of her own. She had ten well-armed and well-equipped galleons, which had been used to protect the treasure convoys crossing the Atlantic. The conquest of Portugal had given her a useful squadron of a further ten galleons. In addition, there were four large ships, called galleasses, brought from Philip's kingdom in Naples. The remaining number of ships were to come from many sources. Philip called on Pope Sixtus V for financial as well as spiritual help in amassing an invincible fleet. Sixtus promised a large sum of money to aid the Armada, but he later changed his mind and said that the money would only be given when the Spanish force had actually landed on English soil. This, of course, was of no use to Philip and his officers, who were no doubt angered when the pontiff reneged on the deal.

The assembly of the great fleet had begun in the spring of 1586. By early 1587, there were sixty ships moored at Cadiz harbour in southern Spain. These included all of Philip's royal fleet, plus ships from all parts of the Spanish Empire. In the midst of these preparations, acting on Elizabeth's instructions based on information from her spy network, Francis

Drake mounted a most damaging attack at Cadiz on 29 April 1587, destroying twenty-four ships.

This was a great blow to Philip, but he rallied his shipwrights and began to commandeer ships from every available source. For example, *El Gran Grifon,* the flagship of the Squadron of Hulks, was a large cargo vessel that had been built at

Portrait of Sir Francis Drake from an engraving by John Pine. He was forty-four years old at the time of the Armada, and one of Elizabeth's most able seamen.

Rostock, in east Germany. It had been forcibly taken over by the Spanish at San Lucar in 1587, having docked there with a cargo of timber. Merchant ships, which were usually used to transport foodstuffs etc., were refurbished by adding extra decks at the forecastle and stern to provide high platforms from which soldiers could fire swivel guns. These extra decks made the ships more unwieldy, but the light swivel guns, mounted on the edge of the deck, were a most effective weapon for close-range fighting between sixteenth-century warships.

Altogether 130 ships were assembled. The ships ranged in size from the fast-sailing patache up to the huge flagship *Santa Ana,* of 1,250 tonnes and forty-seven guns. The fleet consisted of: galleons; hulks or urcas – a type of large Mediterranean merchant ship; pataches of sixty tonnes and nine guns

Bronze and iron swivel gun from *La Trinidad Valencera*.

– used for conveying information throughout the fleet; galleys – large Mediterranean oared vessels that could also be fitted with sails; galleasses; ten caravels – small Mediterranean trading vessels; and ten fellucas – small, fast sailing vessels that were propelled by oars.

The ships were arranged in ten squadrons of unequal numbers. The squadrons were called after their place of origin, as in the Squadron of Andalucia, or after the type of boat, as in the Squadron of Hulks. The Levant Squadron was made up entirely of converted merchant ships. *La Trinidad Valencera,* which has since been excavated by marine archaeologists, was a refurbished Venetian merchant ship of the Levant Squadron. Other ships in the Levant Squadron were the *Juliana*, from Naples, *La Lavia*, the squadron's vice-flagship from Venice, and the *Santa Maria de Visõn,* from Ragusa (now Dubrovnik), in the former Yugoslavia. Each squadron had an overall commander and each ship in the squadron had a captain. In total, the Armada fleet carried 29,453 soldiers and mariners, and 2,241 guns of all types and sizes.

It is easy to see that the great Armada which set sail from Lisbon on May 1588 was one of the most ambitious naval undertakings of the sixteenth century, or indeed any century whatever. The plan was to link up with Spain's well-equipped and well-organised army in Flanders, which was under the command of Alexander Farnese, Duke of Parma, the nephew of Philip II. Using these troops would avoid the need to carry a large number of foot soldiers for the entire sea journey. Even by modern military standards the plan to crush England with a large Armada in conjunction with a mighty army would be hazardous to execute. Their ability to mount a successful attack would be hampered by poor communications and inevitable difficulties and delays between naval and land commands. Philip II was aware of the dangers. On 4 September 1587 he had written to the Duke of Parma, who was wary of the plan, 'We are quite aware of the risk which is incurred by sending a heavy fleet in winter through the Channel without a sure harbour, but the various reasons which render this course necessary are sufficient to counterbalance this objection.' The 'various reasons' were underscored by one: religion.

Before the Armada set sail, it was blessed on the island of San Anton in La Coruña harbour. Each and every crew member received a religious medal of pewter or bronze, most of which had the head of Jesus on one side, and the Virgin Mary on the other side.

Philip saw the Armada as a religious enterprise, a battle for the glory of God. He wrote to the commander of the fleet, Medina Sidonia, 'the cause you are defending is so peculiarly His as to give us hope of His help and favour if it is not made unworthy by our sinfulness.' To ensure the good behaviour of all, each soldier and sailor on board ship received a religious medal of copper or pewter, and the whole enterprise was blessed before *La Felicissima Armada,* the most fortunate Armada, as Philip christened it, set sail from Lisbon. To further ensure that nothing should detract from the high-minded nature of the enterprise, in a separate letter to the shipmasters of the Armada, Medina Sidonia warned:

> It is well known what inconvenience and offence to God is caused by the presence of public or private women. I therefore forbid that any be taken on board.

Medina Sidonia wrote to the king that he had discussed the invasion with a friar and that 'He is certain that Our Lord will vouchsafe a great victory to Your Majesty'. This was exactly the reassurance Philip wanted to receive – that the seemingly impossible could and would be achieved.

The Marquis of Santa Cruz did not live to see the departure of the Armada. He died suddenly of typhus on 9 February 1588. Philip immediately looked for a successor and his place as commander of the Armada was reluctantly taken by Don Alonso Perez de Guzman, Duke of Medina Sidonia. His reluctance was based on the fact that he was a military commander, not a naval one – his successes had all been on land. In addition, he suffered from rheumatism and found the damp sea air extremely painful for his condition. However, Philip ignored his pleas, considered him to have the necessary leadership qualities and insisted he assume control of the expedition. So, in spite of all doubts and misgivings, this historic campaign set forth on 21 July 1588.

THE LEADERS OF THE ARMADA

Don Alonso Perez de Guzman, Duke of Medina Sidonia

The Duke of Medina Sidonia (1550–1619) was thirty-eight years old when he was appointed commander of the Armada. He was one of the richest men in Spain, with a large estate and castle at San Lucar – a large port at the mouth of the Guadalquivir River, which led to Seville. It is also said that he owned half of Andalucia. He was awarded the Order of the Golden Fleece, the highest Order of Chivalry in Spain, by Philip II, who held him in great esteem. Normally this Order was restricted to those of royal blood; Philip can be seen wearing his in contemporary portraits. There is only one, rather indistinct, portrait of Medina Sidonia available to us. It is by an unknown painter and is now held in a private collection, but he is described as being heavily built, of middle height with a light-coloured beard and a high forehead.

Medina Sidonia was a military man who had led an army during the successful Portuguese campaign in 1580. He was an excellent administrator and had organised the provisioning and manning of the fleets that sailed regularly between Spain and her colonies in America. The Duke of Parma, the

Venetian ambassador to Madrid and the French ambassador, among many others, all spoke very highly of him. Words such as brave, diligent and careful were used to describe his character.

Medina Sidonia's later actions showed that he was a considerate and caring leader, who had tried in every way to make a success of the venture. His reluctance to undertake command of the Armada was based on sound reasons: his previous successes had all been on land and, as he had already been involved in the preparations, he knew that the organisation of the fleet and its provisions was in a state of disarray. Medina Sidonia also knew that the enterprise would cost him a great deal of money because leaders were expected to use their personal wealth to fund the expedition. (In the event, he had to spend three-quarters of a million ducats of his own personal fortune, both in the preparation of the Armada and also to relieve the sick and starving soldiers and sailors at Santander on their return home.) His wife encouraged him not to take on the task, telling him

DUCATS
The ducat was a Venetian gold trade coin of standard size and value, used throughout Europe, rather like the modern Euro.

that he had sufficient fame and standing as owner of his estates at San Lucar. More significantly, in a second letter to the king, written on 16 February 1588, he said that the enterprise was ill-conceived and he felt it had little chance of success: 'The force is so great, and the undertaking so important that it would not be right for a person like myself, possessing no experience of seafaring or war, to take charge of it.'

However, Philip was ill at this time and Medina Sidonia's second letter was intercepted by two councillors of state and never given to the king. They replied to him: 'We dare not show his Majesty what you have just written ... Do not depress us with fears for the fate of the Armada, because in such a cause God will make sure it succeeds.'

Medina Sidonia had no choice; he was prevailed upon to command the enormous fleet. He set forth as captain of the *San Martin*, the flagship of the Squadron of Portugal, a ship of 1,000 tonnes and forty-eight guns.

Alexander Farnese, Duke of Parma

The Duke of Parma (1545–1592) was the son of Philip's sister. He had taken part in the famous victory of Lepanto in 1571 against the Ottoman Turks, and was only thirty-two years of age when he became general of the army in Flanders, where he proved himself a very able commander. His troops were recruited from Spain, Italy, Germany and Burgundy, and they were recognised as the best fighting force in Europe.

Parma had visited England in his youth, making him one of the

Alexander Farnese, Duke of Parma, from an engraving by John Pine. He was Philip's commander of the military forces and governor of the Netherlands from 1578.

few Armada commanders who had done so. His great personal wealth came from his inheritance as ruler of his Italian state. His royal connections, coupled with his great wealth, made him a very influential leader.

Before the Armada sailed, Philip informed Medina Sidonia that although he had control of the entire fleet, when the land and sea forces met at Flanders, the Duke of Parma was to assume overall command. This was not altogether a happy arrangement; the aged Santa Cruz, Medina Sidonia's predecessor, had objected to these conditions before his death.

Don Alonso Martinez de Leiva

Don Alonso (c.1555–1588) was a nobleman and commander of the carrack *La Rata Santa Maria Encoronada* of the Levant Squadron, and one of the largest ships in the fleet. He was an illustrious volunteer and, in his thirties, one of the youngest leaders. His enthusiasm for the grand enterprise fired many other young men from Spain's noblest and wealthiest houses to volunteer. Highly regarded by his men, he was also a favourite of the king. Secret orders signed by Philip were carried in a locked chest by Juan Martinez de Recalde. These orders gave command of the Armada to de Leiva if Medina Sidonia should perish in battle. Although the experienced and able Recalde was Medina Sidonia's second-in-command and should have been his immediate successor, de Leiva was more nobly born and a favourite of the king.

De Leiva had been awarded the Cross of a Knight of Santiago, one of the highest Orders of Chivalry in the land. He had already served as a military commander in Holland and Portugal, proving himself a fine leader of men. However, his naval experience was confined to galley warfare against Muslim raiders off the shores of Italy; Muslim raiders constantly attacked their Christian enemies in the western Mediterranean from their oared galleys.

There are no known portraits of de Leiva, but a portrait of a Spanish nobleman by El Greco, now in the Montreal Museum of Fine Arts, may possibly be his likeness. His physical appearance was described as tall and slender with fair, smooth hair and pale complexion. In demeanour he was mild and quietly spoken. He proved to be courageous in battle and resourceful in adversity, thinking always of the safety of his men.

Juan Martinez de Recalde

Juan Martinez de Recalde (1526–1588) was the commander of the vice-flagship *San Juan de Portugal*, a 1,000-tonne galleon. He was second-in-command to Medina Sidonia of the entire fleet, and captain of the Squadron of Biscay of fourteen ships. Recalde was the Armada's most experienced naval tactician, whose abilities had been recognised by the king, after a lifetime at sea, with the award of the Order of a Knight of Santiago. He was aged sixty-two at the start of the campaign.

Recalde had taken part in the Spanish conquest of Portugal and had been in charge of some of the large treasure fleets that sailed between Seville and the Americas. Most importantly, he had experienced conditions in the North Atlantic in

1572 and 1575, when he was in command of expeditions sailing between Spain and Flanders. He was also one of the very few Spanish commanders who had any knowledge of the Irish coastline – he had landed the expedition at Smerwick, on the southwest coast of Ireland, in 1580 and had surveyed the coastline at the same time. This knowledge was to be his salvation when his ship was threatened with shipwreck in Blasket Sound, County Kerry.

Diego Flores de Valdes

Diego Flores de Valdes (*c.*1528–1590) was the commander of the Castilian Squadron of sixteen ships. He was the Duke of Medina Sidonia's chief naval adviser and was aged almost sixty at the start of the Armada campaign. Although he was the commander of the Castilian Squadron, as Medina Sidonia's chief naval adviser he sailed on board the flagship *San Martin,* with the Squadron of Portugal.

De Valdes was ruthless and easily enraged and he heartily disliked his cousin, Don Pedro de Valdes, who captained the *Nuestra Senora de la Rosario.* In 1565, on Philip's orders, both he and his cousin had sailed to secure Spanish interests in Florida, where a group of Huguenots had fled after the St Bartholomew's Day massacre of Protestants in France. Although the Huguenot settlers surrendered and expected to be treated fairly, they were all killed; it is thought that de Valdes ordered the execution. It is often suggested that it was he who gave the order that if any ship left her assigned place in battle formation, her captain was to be hanged. Even though this command was obviously unfair and unrealistic in the heat of battle, the unfortunate captain of the *Santa Barbara*, Don Cristobal de Avila, was given no mercy and was hanged on 11 August 1588. De Valdes was not popular with either the men or the ships' officers, many of whom resented what they saw as his undue influence over Medina Sidonia.

The Spanish Fleet

The leaders described above are the Armada's most illustrious characters, and also the men we know most about. However, there were ten squadrons in all and ten squadron leaders. The full list is as follows.

SQUADRON	FLAGSHIP	SQUADRON LEADER
Squadron of Portugal	*San Martin*	Duke of Medina Sidonia (and overall commander of the Armada)
Squadron of Biscay	*Santa Ana*	Juan Martinez de Recalde
Squadron of Castile	*San Cristobal*	Diego Flores de Valdes
Squadron of Andalucia	*Nuestra Senora de la Rosario*	Don Pedro de Valdes
Squadron of Guipuzcoa	*Santa Ana*	Don Miguel de Oquendo
Levant Squadron	*La Regazona*	Martin de Bertendona
Squadron of Hulks	*El Gran Grifon*	Juan Gomez de Medina
Squadron of the Kingdom of Naples	*San Lorenzo*	Don Hugo de Moncada
Pataches and Zabras	These were small boats and did not have a flagship	Don Antonio Hurtado de Mendoza
Galleys		The four galleys in the fleet were under the command of Diego de Medrano

PART TWO

The Journey to England

SHIPS OF THE ARMADA

The Spanish Galleon

Galleons were sixteenth-century ships used by both sides in the English–Spanish conflict. The prototype galleon was first built in England, and some seventeen years later the pattern was copied by the Spanish and other European powers.

The typical Spanish galleon was a heavily armed, two-decked craft with high stern and forecastle and a beaked prow. They were carvel-built, which means the outer planks were laid edge-to-edge and held together by iron nails. These ships could be up to fifty metres in length and measure ten metres at the widest part. They had three to four masts set with narrow, triangular sails known as lateen sails. The height and weight of the masts – they were up to twenty-two metres high – meant that the ships had to carry large amounts of ballast (usually large stones) for stability. The wreck-site of the *Juliana,* one of the fleet's galleons, yielded a rudder measuring twelve metres. The galleon had a large hold because it was necessary to carry plenty of provisions on long voyages. It had one gun-deck set high above the waterline. Each ship

An engraving by John Pine, which shows a galleon in the foreground under attack from the English.

was required to have up to four anchors, which were slung along the side of the ship near the bow.

The high forecastle and stern, plus the large hold and the need to carry both soldiers and sailors, slowed the galleon's progress and left it at a disadvantage when in conflict with the swifter and more manoeuvrable English ships.

Probably the best representations of the Armada galleons are provided by the illustrations of the English engraver John Pine. Lord Howard, the English commander, commissioned the weaver Francis Spiernig of Brussels to create a series of tapestries telling the story of the Armada campaign, after the English success. These were completed about 1595 and were hung in the English House of Lords in 1650, where they remained until they were destroyed by fire in 1834. Fortunately, Pine had produced ten engravings taken from the tapestries. These engravings were published in 1739.

Although the galleon was originally designed by the English, Lord Howard realised that the high forecastle caught the wind, slowed the ship and made her difficult to manoeuvre in bad weather. The design was therefore modified to eliminate this effect. The English boats sat lower in the water and, as Medina Sidonia wrote in his diary, 'their ships being very nimble and of such good steerage, they did with them whatsoever they desired'. The Spanish, however, kept to the original design, so their ships were slower and more cumbersome. It is estimated that in fair winds the galleon's speed was four to six knots, which is approximately four nautical miles an hour. The English ships were not much faster than this, but they were much more easily manoeuvred.

The Spanish Galleass

Four galleasses (the sum total of galleasses in the Armada fleet) made up the Squadron from the Kingdom of Naples, under the command of Don Hugo de Moncado. They were the flagship *San Lorenzo*, the *Zuniga*, the *Girona* and the *Napolitana*.

The galleass was intended to be a cross between an oared galley and a galleon. The oared galley was a common ship type in the Mediterranean. Although large and slow-moving, it was capable of movement without the necessity for sails. The galleon, though swifter, was reliant on wind-power for movement. By combining the best features of both ship types it was hoped to produce a doubly efficient ship, but the reality was quite different. Galleasses had performed the useful function of supply ships at the Battle of Lepanto, off western Greece, in 1582, when they had fought on the Christian side against the Ottoman Armada. They had performed well in the Ionian Sea, but in the Atlantic conditions they encountered off western Europe, they proved unwieldy and unreliable.

Detail from a Pine engraving showing galleasses. There are few contemporary illustrations of galleasses. Note the number of oars protruding from the rowing-deck.

Galleasses were very large ships. Their average weight was 600 tonnes, they had three masts and were very heavily armed, for example, the *Girona* is reputed to have had fifty cannon on board. A large iron-shod ram protruded from the bow of each vessel. The rowers were employed to manoeuvre the ship into close-range battle position. Eighteen to twenty-two rowers on each side could not move these boats very fast, even in ideal conditions. In the stormy seas they encountered around England and Ireland, the galleasses were very cumbersome indeed.

Although illustrations of galleasses are rare, we have additional details of their appearance from contemporary accounts. In 1530, a decree of the Venetian senate ruled that every galleass had to be forty-seven metres long, have a beam of eight metres and have a space between decks of 3.20 metres. Pietro Martire d'Anghirera, who sailed in a galleass at the beginning of the sixteenth century, recorded that it had 150 oarsmen seated in rows of twenty-five in tiers on each side of the ship. Fifty sailors were employed to handle the running rigging from the decks, while twelve others climbed along the yards to take in sail when required. (The yardarm is a large wooden spar crossing the mast horizontally from which the sails are set.) These twelve sailors also handled the large rudders, which were susceptible to damage in heavy seas. An Englishman, Richard Tomson, who boarded the *San Lorenzo* after it ran aground at Calais, described it as having red oars and sails. The upper decks of this ship were also red and the rowers all wore red jackets. This was unusual, as even the sailors did not have regular uniforms.

There was a striking contrast between the facilities enjoyed by the noble commanders and captains of the Armada and the ordinary soldier and sailor.

The Cross of a Knight of St John of Jerusalem set on top of three large gold chains. The largest of these chains is 230cm long and weighs almost one kilogram. The cross is made of gold that has been keyed to contain white enamel, a small amount of which still remains despite 400 years on the seabed. *Girona.*

The Spanish nobility on board dressed with the same luxurious splendour as if they were attending court, complete with gold buttons, gold chains, gold rings, Orders of Chivalry and glittering diamond rings. Each ship's captain wore a large gold chain over his shirt and under his outer clothing. The largest gold chain recovered from the *Girona* weighs just under a kilo and is likely to have been a chain of this type. Their clothing was of silk and velvet with shoes of the finest leather. Spanish fashion was dominant in western Europe at the time of the Armada, and the styles were reflected even in

England. Men wore a doublet, trunk hose and short cloak or sleeveless coat. The doublet was a close-fitting padded jacket that fastened at the centre front from neck to pointed waist. It had a tight, high collar. Basques hid the points or ties that fastened the trunk hose to the doublet. Trunk hose were single garments consisting of padded breeches and long, tailored

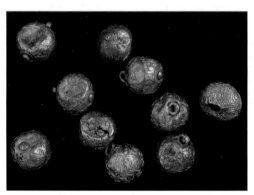

stockings sewn together. Knee breeches with separate stockings were also worn from about 1570 onwards. Buttons had been used since the fourteenth century, but by the sixteenth century they were a focus for male extravagance – rows of them were sewn closely together in large numbers. The wealthy

In later life, Philip II was an austere and devout man, plain in his dress and ornament, but this was not reflected by the members of his court, either in garments or in jewellery. Buttons were used extensively on fashionable dress of the sixteenth century and wealthy noblemen would own many precious sets. These gold buttons came from the *Girona*.

nobleman would own many precious sets of buttons, so it is not surprising that gold buttons were among the treasures found on the *Girona*.

The officers' quarters on the upper decks were splendidly furnished with fine tables and chairs. They dined off silver and silver gilt plates and ate with silver forks and spoons. Food was served on fine pewter plates and goblets and silver jugs held their wine. Unlike their below-deck colleagues, their food was not subject to rationing. In the evening, light

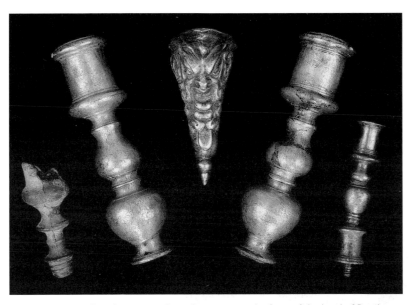

These silver candlesticks, tapersticks and jug spout in the form of the head of Bacchus, the Greek god of wine, were part of a range of decorated silver tableware pieces from the *Girona*.

was provided by candles held in silver, pewter and copper candlesticks, and also by wooden lanterns with glass sides. For entertainment they could play musical instruments or play shipboard games with wooden balls.

To protect them from the dreadful stenches that came from below the gun-decks, the ships' officers carried silver perfume flasks with little crystal droppers, which they could use to mask the repellent smells. Gold ear- and toothpicks and fine-toothed wooden combs were used to keep

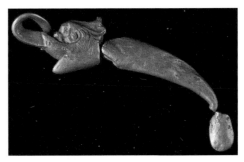

A gold ear- and toothpick in the shape of a dolphin. The dolphin was a popular decorative motif on board ship. A small silver dolphin mount and several bronze mounts were also found at the *Girona* wreck-site.

themselves as clean and neat as possible, even in the heat of battle.

Life for the ordinary soldier and seaman was less grand, although they did get paid each month (*see* caption below). Their dishes and jugs were made of pottery or wood and their eating utensils were of pewter or wood. They did not have

forks but made do by cutting up their food with their daggers. Each man had a wine-skin, made from goat-skin, with a wooden mouthpiece and stopper. These were worn slung from a belt and a reviving draught could be snatched in the smoke and heat of battle.

The following was the payment received by a Spanish soldier or sailor per month: gold one escudo piece of Joanna and Carolus, Seville mint; gold four escudo piece of Philip II, Seville mint; gold two escudo piece of Philip II, Seville mint; gold two escudo piece of Philip II, Granada mint; silver five Tari piece of the Kingdom of the Two Sicilies.

The food rations for each man seem quite generous when we read Medina Sidonia's instructions to the shipmasters of the Armada at Lisbon, on 21 April 1588:

> Two flesh days, Sundays and Thursdays – each man allowed 6 ounces of bacon and 2 oz of rice; Mondays and Tuesdays 6 oz cheese and 3 oz of beans or chick peas, and on the three 'fish' days 6 oz of tunny or cod, or 6oz of squid, or five sardines, with 3 oz of beans or chick peas, an ounce and a half of oil and ¼ pint of vinegar.

Pewter plate, wooden bowl and spoon, pottery jug, pewter goblet and pewter jug. The ordinary sailor and infantryman would have used wooden plates, dishes and spoons and simple glazed pottery, while the ships' officers had pewterware of the finest quality.

Each man was allotted 1.5lb of biscuits each day and approximately one bottle of wine. The men cooked together in groups of seven or eight in the brick-built cooking place or galley, which was situated in the centre of the ship. Wood and pine cones were used as fuel and wooden bellows kept the fires going. A lead-lined aperture allowed the smoke to escape up through the boat. The cooking pots were made of copper and were hung over the fires on copper hooks. The cooking areas were kept clean by sweeping with straw whisks.

Spanish musketeer drinking from a wineskin. We know about their clothing from finds made at the wreck-site of *La Trinidad Valencera*. He is carrying a sword belt and a wooden gunpowder flask.

The men's clothing was made of wool and their shoes were leather, although sometimes they wore rough rope sandals. There was none of the splendid personal ornaments worn by the nobility on board; the crew's clothing was strictly functional. Their lives were a constant round of daily tasks. When they were not working on the upkeep of the ship, they would drop a fishing line over the side to get some fresh food to add to their rather monotonous diet. They would also have attended religious services, conducted by the Jesuit priests who Philip had decreed should sail with the Armada. Medina Sidonia gave orders that prayers were to be said twice daily.

Even lower in rank than the soldiers and sailors were the unfortunates who made up the rowing teams. They were either convicted criminals or slaves captured from the colonies. The rowing benches were situated beneath the gundecks, so the rowers were in a terrifying position during the fighting. They were chained to their benches to prevent escape, but that meant they had no chance of survival if the ship sank. They were also confined in the most unhygienic conditions, near to all the noxious smells and unhealthy gases that came up from the bilges of the ship.

NAVAL NAVIGATION IN THE SIXTEENTH CENTURY
Navigators of the sixteenth century had few instruments to assist them. There were few maps of the world and those that did exist were very inaccurate. Navigational aids were also

meagre – navigational charts, navigational dividers, astrolabes, sounding leads and, more rarely, astronomical compendia were available, but the Armada sailors were mostly sailing in uncharted seas. Only Juan Martinez de Recalde had some knowledge of the Irish coastline as he had

Bronze astrolabes were used in the sixteenth century for measuring the angle between the sun and the horizon, which allowed sailors to calculate the ship's latitude. It was one of the most important navigational aids available to the Armada sailors.

landed the ill-fated Smerwick expedition in 1580.

The astrolabe was one of their chief aids. It was a circular, bronze instrument with graduations in degrees marked around the circle. An arm, or alidade, pivoted in the centre of two crossbars. The astrolabe was hung from a ring at the top, and the arm was used to measure the angle of the sun above the horizon at noon. From this information, the ship's latitude could be calculated using astronomical tables.

Sounding leads were heavy, cone-shaped pieces of lead with a concave base and a perforation at the top through which a long cord was threaded. The base was filled with tallow (melted down animal fat) and the sounding lead was let down over the side of the ship to gauge the depth of water and also to ascertain if the seabed was sandy or rocky. If it was sandy, silt would stick to the tallow and its composition would be compared with that noted on the sea chart. The depth of water under the ship was determined by the length of line, which was measured by the sailor's arm span, commonly six feet or 1.8 metres – a measurement still in use today.

Sandglasses were used for measuring distance and speed, and compasses were also available for the Spanish navigator. Remains of the top and bottom of a sandglass and the base of a wooden compass were recovered from *La Trinidad Valencera* (*see* below).

Another aid to successful navigation was the sailor's own knowledge of the winds, sun and stars; the astronomical position of the sun and stars had been known by navigators from earliest times. They knew that the east and west were the directions of the sunrise and sunset. They also knew that north and south were determined by the directions of shadows cast by the noonday sun. At night, the stars rise in the east and set in the west. The experienced sailor also knew from which direction prevailing winds blew – the most important aid for a sailing ship. Unfortunately, while many of these aids were of great use in the warm and more familiar waters of the Mediterranean, they were of little assistance in the stormy Atlantic, where visibility was reduced by wind and rain.

Left: base of wooden compass.

Right: navigational aids recovered from the *Girona* included two bronze astrolabes, two sounding leads and six sets of bronze navigational dividers.

Medina Sidonia had taken over all of the preparations for the Armada's departure after the sudden death of Santa Cruz. In May 1588 the great fleet was ready to set sail from Lisbon. But it was not an auspicious start. A storm blew up and the ships were scattered and some of them damaged. The fleet was forced to anchor at La Coruña in Spain until the scattered ships had all been gathered together again, repairs had been made and more provisions had been taken on board. Each man was blessed and given a pewter or copper medallion showing Christ on one side and the Virgin Mary on the other.

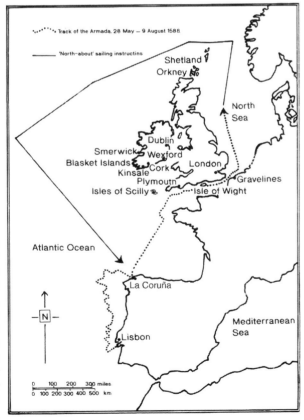

This map shows the route taken by the Armada, from its port of departure at Lisbon in Portugal, until the battles finally ended in the North Sea. Also shown is the route recommended by Medina Sidonia for the fleet's safe return to La Coruña.

Finally, on 21 July 1588, Medina Sidonia was able to lead the Armada out of port and set sail for the invasion and conquest of England.

ENGLAND AWAITS

Throughout her reign, Elizabeth sought to avoid outright conflict by cunning and duplicity. For years she had encouraged her sea rovers – John Hawkins, Francis Drake and others – to attack Spain's convoys and overseas colonies and bring back most of the spoils for her. She always managed to absolve herself from blame by denying any knowledge of the enterprises, although she knighted Drake and Hawkins for their successes in plundering Spain's coffers. This cat-and-mouse game continued for some years until she sent a land army, led by Robert Dudley, Earl of Leicester, into the Netherlands in 1585 to support the Dutch dissidents against Spanish rule. This time she could not deny her significant move against Spain, and it was a major factor in Philip's decision to send his Armada.

The religious conflict between England and Spain that fuelled their enmity had escalated earlier that decade. In 1580, militant Jesuits had arrived in England with the avowed purpose of winning the country back for Catholicism. Although Elizabeth did not actively persecute ordinary Catholics, Jesuit priests were imprisoned and ruthlessly executed in a rising tide of anti-Catholic feeling. Then a Catholic conspiracy was discovered, which aimed to assassinate

Elizabeth upon the arrival of Philip's army in England, and to instate Mary Stuart, Queen of Scots, on the throne; anti-Catholic feeling reached fever pitch. Mary's fate was sealed, the conspirators were hung, drawn and quartered and the threat of the Armada became an ominous reality.

When the Armada eventually appeared off the coast of Plymouth, the English fleet was in a state of readiness for several reasons. Firstly, Elizabeth had no great empire constantly under threat from outsiders to deflect her from her one great purpose: to defend England against Spanish invaders. Secondly, it had been impossible for the Spanish to hide the fact that they were embarking on such a grand enterprise; the English had received frequent dispatches on the Armada's progress from their spy network. Thirdly, in 1578, Sir John Hawkins had replaced Sir William Wynter as Treasurer of the Fleet and had begun a complete overhaul of the English fleet. He replaced the huge, heavy ships, overloaded with soldiers, with race-built, low, comparatively fast ships designed to fight long-range warfare.

This reorganisation of the navy had been fuelled as much by a desire to defend England against the Armada, as it was by a desire to have efficient ships able to attack and plunder Spanish treasure fleets and Spanish ports. As well as employing the services of master shipwrights Peter Pett and Matthew Baker to this end, Sir Henry Cecil, Lord Burghley, Elizabeth's chief naval adviser, commanded the Lord Admiral to order a census of all merchant ships, including the names and addresses of all ships' captains, sailors and indeed anyone useful who was connected with the sea. This was an extremely valuable exercise because it meant the navy would be able to take over merchant ships and obtain crews at short notice in the event of an emergency.

A letter sent to Elizabeth, written on 7 May 1588, from an Italian ship's captain who was serving in the Spanish fleet, revealed that the Armada was ready to depart on that date from Cadiz, and that the soldiers and sailors had all received two months' pay in advance. He informed her that the ship on which he was travelling, *La Rata Santa Maria Encoronada,* had on board Don Alonso de Leiva, with a company of 700 soldiers and 150 sailors. He also told Elizabeth that there were seventy-three very large ships, four galleasses and two galleys, and that in total there were 125 to 130 ships in the fleet. So the English were well aware of the challenge approaching them.

But even this forewarning did not prepare them for the awesome sight of the Spanish Armada when it first sailed into view on 29 July 1588 – such a large fleet had never been seen before. It was first seen about 160 kilometres off Plymouth, at a point called the Lizard, the most southerly point of England. A contemporary account by W. Camden (1551–1623), the English historian and antiquarian, described the Spanish fleet as follows:

> ... with lofty turret-like castle in front, - arranged like a half moon, the wings thereof spreading out about the length of seven miles, sailing very slowly with full sails, the wind being, as it were overrid with carrying them, and the ocean groaning under their weight.

This majestic description is supported by Sir Francis Drake in his account of the first sighting of the Armada:

> ... they cannot be fewer than one hundred and fifty Ships of all Sorts; and severall of them called Galleons and Galleasses, are of a Size never seene before in our Seas, and appeare on the Surface of the Water like floatinge Castles.

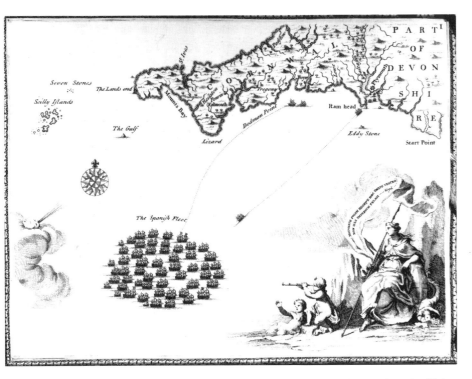

The awesome sight of the Spanish fleet, seen by the English for the first time from the Lizard in Wales. Taken from an engraving by John Pine.

PART THREE

The Battle Begins

BATTLE FORMATIONS AND FIGHTING TECHNIQUES

Although the Spanish had only 130 ships in comparison with 197 gathered together by the English, approximately sixty on both sides were the largest and the most efficient fighting ships. The English had the advantage of being faster and better armed and since they had not already made a long sea voyage before any engagement, their men were also in better physical condition. The Spanish ships, as well as being slower, were also hampered by the amount of supplies they had to carry on a return sea voyage lasting several months.

The Spanish Armada sailed in close crescent formation, which was an effective defensive tactic. The best fighting ships were placed at the points of the crescent and the less able ones in the middle. The English fleet, under the command of the Lord

Charles, Lord Howard of Effingham, Elizabeth's Lord Admiral. Taken from an engraving by John Pine.

Admiral, Charles, Lord Howard of Effingham, decided not to meet them head on as the Spaniards had hoped. The Spanish preferred to fight at close range, damaging the rigging of enemy ships with their short-range swivel guns, fire-pots and shrapnel weapons. Their tactic was to pull the enemy ship alongside with grappling hooks and then send in their well-trained and well-armed soldiers to capture the ship. However, Effingham knew that his best advantage lay in the fact that his ships were faster and that they had more long-range guns. English guns were set on four-wheeled gun carriages, which made them easier to manoeuvre on board than the two-wheeled carriages used by the Spanish. The English tactic was to do as much damage as possible to the enemy with long-range cannon fire. Effingham

Anti-personnel weapon consisting of pieces of metal surrounding an explosive charge. This was recovered from *La Trinidad Valencera*.

decided to split up his fleet and attack on several sides: one section under his own command while the other, under Sir Francis Drake, followed at a distance and attacked when the opportunity arose. So each fleet was intent on pursuing a very different course of action as they drew closer to battle.

THE SEA BATTLES

The first engagement in the English Channel resulted in the Spanish losing two ships, one of which, the *Nuestra Senora de la Rosario,* was accidentally rammed by another Spanish ship in the confusion. The *San Salvador* blew up – this may have been an accident since the presence of so much gunpowder on board a wooden ship was a constant hazard. Don Pedro de Valdes's *Nuestra Senora de la Rosario* was abandoned to her fate and captured on 1 August by English sailors , who gleefully shared out the 50,000 gold ducats they found on board. However, eventually half this sum was recovered and handed over to Elizabeth.

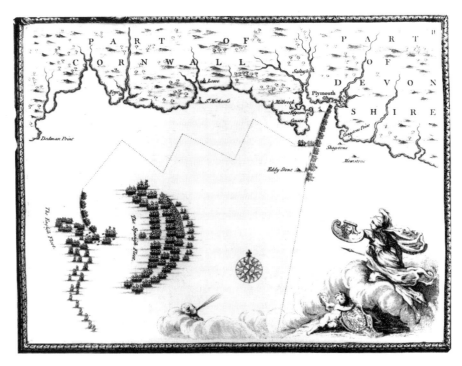

The rival English and Spanish fleets drawn up in battle formation. From an engraving by John Pine.

On the morning of 2 August the Armada was near Portland Bill, sailing to the north of the English fleet. With the

English to their rear, Medina Sidonia decided to turn and attack. While this was happening, the four galleasses, under the command of Don Hugo de Moncado, attacked six of the English ships. The *Ark Royal* and the *San Martin*, Medina Sidonia's ship, came to their aid and *La Trinidad Valencera* also joined in. Much gunfire was exchanged, but relatively little damage was sustained by the Spanish. As the wind shifted, giving the English the advantage, the Spanish broke off and reformed.

On 3 August both fleets were off the Isle of Wight and several long gun battles took place. The English attempted to pick off several Spanish ships that had got left behind. Medina Sidonia managed to drive off the attacks and gave the signal to disengage and reform.

Spanish galleons under attack and damaged by the English fleet.
From an engraving by John Pine.

A council of war was held by the English side and Lord Howard decided to divide his fleet into four squadrons, one under his command, the others under Drake, Hawkins and Frobisher. He realised that attacks on the crescent formation of the Spanish fleet would be more effective if they followed at a distance and attacked when the opportunity arose. Meanwhile, Medina Sidonia realised that attempts to force the English to fight at close quarters were futile and he sent to Parma for fresh supplies of ammunition.

On 5 August, Medina Sidonia sent another message to Parma, repeating his requests for supplies and for confirmation that Parma's troops were ready to join the battle; they were waiting on the Netherlands coast near Dunkirk. The plan was to load Parma's troops onto barges and sail them through the shallow waters to where the waiting galleons were anchored. But there was a problem – Dutch rebels controlled the Flanders coastline and they were waiting to attack in their small, well-armed ships that could sail swiftly in the shallow waters.

HELLBURNERS: THE WATERSHED IN THE BATTLE

On 6 August, the Armada was in sight of the French coast near Boulogne and continued towards Calais, anchoring there in the evening. After conferring with his commanders, Medina Sidonia decided to remain at Calais until he had some news from Parma. The next day a messenger from Parma brought the unwelcome report that he had still not

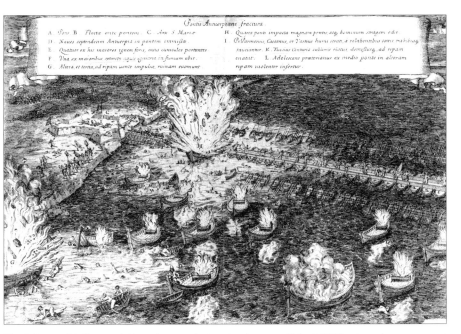

The infamous 'Hellburners'. Here they are depicted at Antwerp, 5 April 1585, where they were used against the Spanish with such devastating results. (National Maritime Museum, London)

started to embark his men or ammunition, and that it would probably be another fortnight before he could set sail. The English took their chance. On 7 August, they sent in eight burning ships, which the Spanish mistakenly thought were the infamous 'Hellburners' – small boats filled with gunpowder, which acted like floating bombs and could wreak tremendous destruction on wooden ships As these 'Hellburners' had already been used by the Dutch against the Spanish with

HELLBURNERS

The 'Hellburner' had been designed by an Italian, Federico Giambelli, who provided his services for several European powers. Giambelli had previously worked for the Dutch rebels, but at that time it was rumoured that he was working for Elizabeth. Even in the sixteenth century, arms manufacturers sold their weapons to the highest bidder.

devastating effect at Antwerp, they were right to be afraid.

Panicked by the oncoming blazing fireships, the Armada captains ordered their ships to cut anchor and the ships scattered – for the first time losing their defensive crescent formation. The galleass *San Lorenzo* had its rudder damaged in the confusion and ran aground on a sandbank, where the English were able to capture it the next morning.

While the battles raged between the two sides, Elizabeth showed her strength of character and personal bravery in her stirring speech to the troops at Tilbury, under the command of the Earl of Leicester, on 8 August 1588. Although those on land did not know how the sea battle was going at that time, this was, in fact, the day of the final attack on the Spanish fleet, at Gravelines, and the end of the Spanish threat:

> ... and therefore I am come amongst you, as you see, at this time, not for my recreation and disport, but being resolved, in the midst and heat of battle, to live or die amongst you all, to lay down for my God, and for my kingdom, and for my people, my honour and my blood, even in the dust.
>
> I know I have the body of a weak and feeble woman, but I have the heart and stomach of a king, and of a King of England too, and think foul scorn that Parma or Spain, or any prince of Europe should dare to invade the borders of my realm ... not doubting but by your obedience to my general, by your concord in the camp, and your valour in the field, we shall shortly have a famous victory over these enemies of my God, of my Kingdoms and of my people.

Medina Sidonia attempted to gather his ships together again while being pursued through heavy seas and strong winds by the English. The Battle of Gravelines, off the French coast – the fifth in the invasion – had the most serious consequences. Here both sides got close enough to inflict considerable damage on each other. After many hours fighting a sudden storm separated the two fleets, by which time the English had run out of ammunition. The Spanish had suffered badly – they had lost hundreds of men and most of their large fighting ships had sprung leaks. The strong winds forced the fleet up the North Sea towards Scotland, and two Spanish ships, the *San Juan de Sicilia* and, it is thought, the *Maria Juan*, which had been very badly damaged in the fighting, sank. Dutch rebels captured two other damaged craft, the *San Mateo* and the *San Felipe*, which had drifted onto sandbanks off Flanders. The Dutch killed the ordinary crewmen and soldiers and held the noble officers for ransom.

The remainder of the Armada was also drifting towards the sandbanks, blown by a strong northwest wind. By good fortune, the wind shifted to west-southwest and disaster was averted. The ships were then able to move into the deep waters of the North Sea.

After the Gravelines encounter, which was disastrous for the Spanish, Medina Sidonia was forced to reconsider his position. His ships were too badly damaged to attempt another attack on the English. The decision was made to save as many ships as possible and sail home to Spain.

Medina Sidonia's sailing instructions for the Armada's return to Spain were obtained from a prisoner interrogated later in Ireland. He made every effort to save as many ships and men as possible, and his careful instructions were typical of his character. The route intended for the homeward journey was around the north coast of Scotland and Ireland.

> The Course that is first to be held is to the north north-east until you be found under 61 degrees and a half. And then to take great heed lest you fall upon the island of Ireland for fear of the harm that may happen unto you upon that Coast: Then parting from those island and doubling the cape in 61 degrees and a half you shall come west South-west until you be found under 58 degrees. And from thence to the South-west to the height of 53 degrees and then to the South south-west making to the Cape Finisterre and so to procure your entrance into the Groyne (La Coruña) or to fferoll (Galicia) or to any other port of the Coast of Galicia.

Ships' rations of biscuits, water and wine were reduced throughout the fleet, and on 13 August they started their journey home through rough Atlantic seas, which became progressively worse. Many of the crew were ill through lack of water and inadequate rations.

The autumn storms of 1588 were so exceptionally severe that they were mentioned in the public records. The Elizabethan State Papers speak of the terrible storms on 17 and 18 September 1588. Marcos de Aramburu, who wrote of the sinking of the *Santa Maria de la Rosa,* spoke of 'a most violent storm with a very wild sea' and 'stormy sea with heavy sky and rain'. All in all, conditions which made steering the top-heavy Spanish boats very difficult, and navigation with their limited instruments almost impossible.

LOST AT SEA

The greatest losses sustained by the Armada were caused by the storms and not by the English adversary. Probably over forty ships perished on the return journey, although an accurate number of ships lost is not available. Medina Sidonia managed to keep sixty-seven ships together, some of them his best galleons, and bring them safely home with their sick and starving crews. It has been suggested that some of the embargoed vessels (vessels forcibly appropriated by the Spanish authorities) returned to their home ports in Europe, and not to Spain. Some of the ships were driven towards Ireland by the terrible storms and some sailed there in an attempt to find shelter, fresh food and water. The ships' pilots did their best, but very few had any knowledge of the treacherous Irish coastline and there were no accurate charts available.

By October 1588, it is estimated that over twenty-five ships had been lost off the Irish coastline. The Elizabethan State Papers of Ireland and other contemporary documentary sources list twenty-four ships, but not all their names are known. At present we know the names and positions of twelve Armada wrecks (*see* map, p.81). Although it is not listed, we know that another ship sank off the north coast as well as the galleass *Girona*. It is possible, but not certain, that it was the *Barca de Amburg*. We know that a ship sank off the coast of Tralee, and it may have been the *San Esteban*. The names of the other wrecked ships are not known, and it has never been established exactly where they went down. However, what is known is that several thousand drowned in the crashing Atlantic swell that pounded the fleeing ships, and that the thousands of Spanish men who did manage to reach shore were hardly more fortunate.

Medina Sidonia's stark warning, 'Take great heed lest you fall upon the island of Ireland, for fear of the harm that may happen unto you upon that coast', was to prove an uncanny prophesy.

The wrecking of a Spanish galleon off Port na Spaniagh, by the Belfast artist John Carey. Port na Spaniagh is the location of the wreck-site of the galleass *Girona*. Another ship, the *Castillo Negro*, is also reputed to have been lost off the North Antrim coast.

PART FOUR

The Armada and Ireland

IRELAND IN 1588

From prehistoric times, Ireland had established links with Europe through trade and pilgrimage. A favoured place of pilgrimage for Irish religious orders was Santiago de Compostela in Galicia, northern Spain. The Anglo-Norman settlement of Ireland in the twelfth century gave a boost to European trade, and during that century Galway was an important centre for wine imported from Spain and Portugal. The wine was then distributed to England, Wales and Scotland. There were other European links through the wool trade – large quantities of Irish fleece were exported to Florence, the great wool-producing centre of Italy. Hides and wheat were other important exports, largely to France and England. By the thirteenth and fourteenth centuries, there was a well-established fish trade from Youghal, County Cork, Malahide, County Dublin and County Wexford.

The importance of Ireland both as a trading neighbour and as a strategic naval base was recognised by the English, who feared that continental Europe might conquer Ireland and so gain control of the Atlantic trading routes. England wanted control of the Irish trade routes, especially the financially successful fisheries.

By the 1500s, the most settled part of Ireland was the area around Dublin and the east coast called the Pale, which had been occupied by English settlers. The aim of the English was to extend this control over the rest of the country. But the rest of the country was much less stable, with great lordships ruling in many areas, determined to preserve their 'patch' against all comers. Inter-clan fighting between powerful lords, and cattle-raiding carried on by lesser clan chiefs in the west and northwest of the country, made Ireland a very unsettled place.

When the Anglo-Norman settlers had come to Ireland in the twelfth century, they intermarried with the local population and became supporters of the English Crown. By 1330, the power of the Anglo-Norman lords was at its height. The most powerful of these were the Geraldines, who occupied the Earldom of Desmond in the southwest province of Munster. Although the Geraldines ostensibly gave allegiance to the English Crown in the person of the English Lord Deputy, they were concerned for their own position and the ownership of their lands. They conspired against England when they felt under threat, setting in motion a long history of attack and counter-attack.

The Tudor conquest of Ireland began during the reign of Henry VIII. Various insurrections in Ireland were put down during Henry's reign. After his death in 1547, during the brief reign of his son, Edward VI, efforts continued to establish the

Map of Ireland in 1567, showing the strongholds of the various ruling clans.

Reformation in Ireland by the imposition of Protestant ritual and bishops. This was greeted with hostility by the Catholic clergy. However, the restoration of Catholicism under Henry's daughter, Mary Tudor, had a calming effect. But when Elizabeth I ascended to the throne in 1556, she again sought to impose Protestantism on the land. In 1560, she was declared the Supreme Governor of the Church of Ireland and attempted to impose religious uniformity throughout Ireland. Civil and religious courts were set up to reinforce her command.

But large parts of Ireland remained free of English control. Elizabeth's strategy was to send in large numbers of English and Scottish settlers who would support the English Church and government in Ireland. Considerable numbers of English and Scots were granted large tracts of land in the country. The settlers treated the indigenous inhabitants badly and were loathed by them in return.

On the continent, Irish exiles won the support of Pope Sixtus V to land an invasion force in Ireland. In October 1580, the Spanish landed a mixed force of 800 Spanish and Italian volunteers and occupied the fort at Smerwick, west of Dingle in County Kerry. The incursors had expected local support, but this did not happen. The entire company surrendered to the English forces, thinking it was the safest thing to do. They were all massacred, with the exception of fifteen, who were held for ransom by a force under the command of the Lord Deputy Lord Grey de Wilton and Sir Walter Raleigh. This brutal treatment was to be repeated against the survivors of

Bronze mortar and pestle from *La Trinidad Valencera*.
This may have been used in the preparation of medicines or foodstuffs.

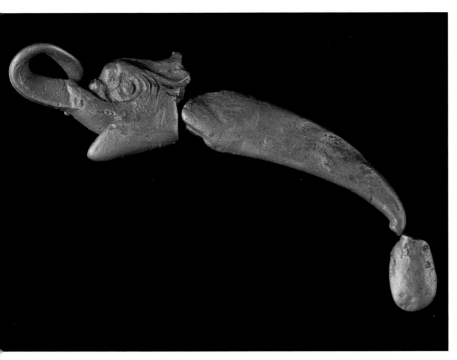

Gold ear- and toothpick in the shape of a dolphin.
The tail was used as the earpick; the nose was used as the toothpick.
This type of instrument was common in the sixteenth and early seventeenth centuries.

Left: Twelve portrait cameos of Caesars in lapis lazuli, gold, enamel and pearls were recovered from the *Girona*. This is the twelfth cameo, discovered some thirty years after the original excavation. The Roman emperor depicted on it may be Domitian or Trajan.

Below: Gold salamander pendant set with rubies. The salamander was a mythical lizard able to survive and extinguish fire, which made it an appropriate talisman to wear on board a wooden fighting ship. Only three of the original set of nine rubies still survive. Rubies were available commercially in the sixteenth century from Burma, Thailand, Cambodia, Ceylon and Afghanistan (also the centre for the lapis lazuli used for the cameo portraits). Their presence in this splendid jewel further reflects the grandeur and outreach of the Spanish Empire. *Girona.*

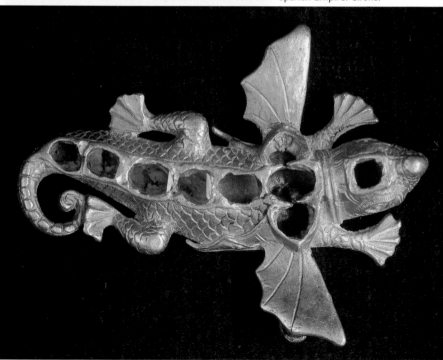

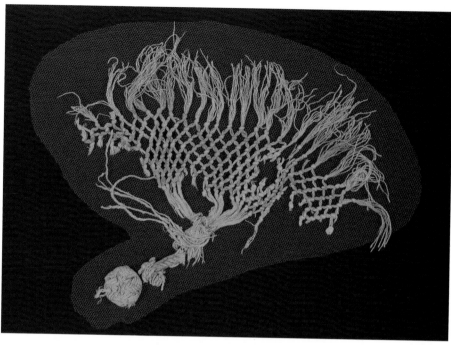

Gold silk tassel recovered from *La Trinidad Valencera*.
This may have hung from the belt of a Spanish musketeer.

The beautiful gold-and-blue enamel earring of the Madonna and Child.
For a full description of this jewel, *see* p.119.

Above: Jewels and coins which had belonged to the noble Spanish officers who perished in the wreck of the *Girona*.

Left: Silver crucifix heavily abraded by the sea. A gold cross, silver crucifix, bronze cross and lead cross were all found at the *Girona* wreck-site, underlining the fact that the Armada was a religious enterprise.

Above: Gold one escudo and two escudo pieces from the *Girona*.

Right: Wooden bellows from *La Trinidad Valencera*, which would have been used to fan the cooking fires in the galley on board ship.

Copper buckets were used for holding water to sluice down the decks. More importantly, they were also on hand for dipping a goatskin-covered sponge head, which was used to clean any burning material from inside the gun barrels before the next charge was inserted. Copper was safe to use near gunpowder because it produced no sparks. *La Trinidad Valencera.*

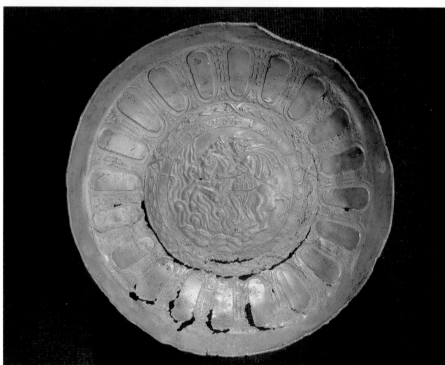

Small metal bowl commemorating the victory of the Marquis of Santa Cruz on the Portuguese island of Terceira, in the Azores, in 1583. In the centre is the figure of St James on horseback, riding on billowing waves. The Latin inscription around the figure translates as: For fatherland and friendship.

Right: A delicate piece of gold filigree, which was folded in two when found. It was probably a decorative end for a silk tie fastening. *Girona*.

Below: One section of a composite gold chain set with two pearls and a central ruby. Two sections of this chain were recovered from the *Girona*. Large bejewelled chains like this can be seen in contemporary portraits.

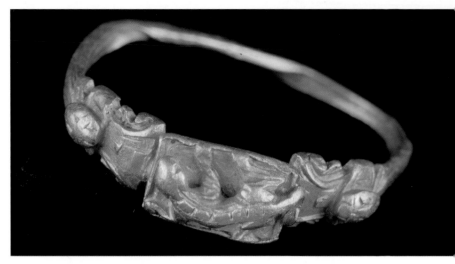

A gold ring with a salamander on the bezel, flanked by two small human heads. In the sixteenth century, Spanish goldsmiths created many jewels in the shape of exotic animals, influenced in part by the splendid gold ornaments made by South American craftsmen. The head was frequently depicted by pre-Hispanic Indian goldsmiths on pectoral, nose and ear ornaments. *Girona*.

Astrolabes were used by navigators for measuring the angle between the sun and the horizon in order to calculate the ship's latitude. When in working use, an alidade or sight-rule would pivot in the centre where the crossbars meet. The calibrations on the ring have been obliterated by sea action, but the remains of its suspension loop can be seen at the top. This astrolabe was found at the wreck-site of the *Girona*.

the Armada shipwrecks of 1588.

The Smerwick landing was part of a general rebellion in Munster by the leaders of the Geraldines in the Earldom of Desmond. The troops of Gerald FitzGerald, 14th Earl of Desmond, were unable to withstand the English onslaught and he was forced to retreat while his castles were systematically overthrown, one by one, until he was killed in Kerry on 11 November 1583. The English forces then turned on the local rebels and it is estimated that over 30,000 were killed or starved to death in this conflict. As well as destroying property, the English forces also destroyed crops, reducing the population to starvation and poverty.

In 1588, when the Armada ships were either being shipwrecked or attempting to land to procure supplies, many areas were under direct control of the English forces. In 1588 there were approximately 2,000 troops in Ireland. These troops were a mixture of English soldiers and Irish and Scots mercenaries. It was only in the northern part of Ireland, in the counties of Antrim, Down, Tyrone, Fermanagh and Donegal, that strong opposition to English rule still existed. There, leaders such as the O'Neills, O'Donnells and MacSweeneys had well-organised, armed followers to defend their lands against the English. The English rightly feared that the Spanish survivors would join with the Irish rebels opposed to them.

This, then, was the uneasy situation in Ireland in which the Spanish survivors found themselves. When the new Lord Deputy, Sir William Fitzwilliam, arrived in Dublin in 1588, he decreed that it was the duty of every loyal citizen 'to apprehend and execute all Spaniards found of what quality soever'.

THE FATE OF THE ARMADA

'Take great heed lest you fall upon the island of Ireland ...'

The large refurbished Venetian merchant ship *La Trinidad Valencera*, captained by Don Alonso de Luzon, was the first Armada ship to run aground. It hit a reef in Kinnagoe Bay, at Malin Head in north Donegal, on 16 September 1588. De Luzon managed to hire a boat from the O'Doherty clan at the vastly inflated price of 200 ducats so that he could get his men off the stricken ship before it broke up. Once on shore, he attempted to march them to a castle where, he had been told, there was a sympathetic Irish bishop named Cornelius. When they got there, they were met by a much larger force of Irish mercenaries under English command and there were several minor clashes. De Luzon was persuaded that if he and his men laid down their arms they would be taken to the Lord Deputy in Dublin. Supposing that this was the best way of saving his men, de Luzon did so. The company was then systematically robbed of everything they had, including their clothes. The following morning, de Luzon and some of his nobles worth saving for ransom were separated from the others, who were herded into a field and massacred with lead shot and lances. Over 300 Spaniards were killed that morning, but about 150 managed to escape to the castle of

Bishop Cornelius, who helped them to reach the coast and get a boat to Scotland. De Luzon and his officers were marched to Drogheda.

About 100 wealthy Spaniards were held in Dublin Castle and in Drogheda, on the Lord Deputy's orders. A group of thirty were sent to England on board a pinnace, *The Swallow*, to continue ransom negotiations with Spain. (A pinnace was a small vessel of twenty tonnes, carrying both oar and sail and used to take messages swiftly throughout the fleet.) But the Spanish prisoners overpowered the crew of nine and sailed the boat to La Coruña. There the English crew were all hanged.

During the storm of 21 September 1588, the *San Juan de Portugal*, captained by Recalde, and the *San Juan Bautista*, captained by Marcos de Aramburu, managed to anchor in Great Blasket Sound off County Kerry – a notoriously dangerous place with undersea reefs. Recalde's ship was fortunate to ride out the storm and return to Spain safely. (Recalde was the captain who had landed the expedition at Smerwick and surveyed the Irish coast at the same time.) The *San Juan Bautista* did not

This Armada motto, a detail from the Pine engravings, translates as *In the end the good cause triumphs 1588*.

fare so well. It sank, although Recalde managed to collect some of the survivors and salvage some of the guns before setting sail for Spain. He arrived at La Coruña with a much depleted crew. He had lost 170 sick and starving men on the journey home and the rest were in very bad shape. Recalde, too, was very ill by this time and unable to walk ashore. He died nine days later at the age of sixty-two. His contribution to the Armada had been great and his bravery in battle and skills as a commander had been one of its greatest assets.

Marcos de Aramburu was the captain and paymaster of the Castilian Squadron, and from the deck of Recalde's ship he was able to give a first-hand account of the fate of the *Santa Maria de la Rosa*. She was the vice-flagship of the Guipuzcoa Squadron, a vessel of 945 tonnes, carrying 250 men and armed with twenty-six guns. She had been holed four times, but when a reef at the neck of Blasket Sound tore out the bottom of the ship, she sank in a terrifyingly short space of time. Marcos de Aramburu was later to describe it in 'An Account of what happened to Marcos de Aramburu, controller and paymaster of the galleons of Castile in the vice-flagship of those under his charge':

> In an instant we saw she was going to the bottom while trying to hoist the foresail, and immediately she went down with the whole crew, not a soul escaping – a most extraordinary and terrible occurrence.

There was actually one survivor, Giovanni de Manona, the fourteen-year-old son of the ship's pilot. He was interrogated by the English, but his eventual fate is unknown. It is not thought to have been a happy one.

Another unnamed vessel ran aground off the coast of Tralee, County Kerry, and twenty-five of the crew gave themselves up. After interrogation by the English authorities, all were executed. A Scottish mercenary named McLaughlan MaCabe boasted of killing, with his axe, eighty survivors from a ship that had been wrecked off Tralee, perhaps the same ship. Weakened by illness, lack of food and seasickness, the survivors had little chance of defending themselves.

Three other ships attempted to anchor off Streedagh Strand, County Sligo, but they were gradually pounded to pieces by the fierce seas. In his letter to Philip II, Francisco de Cuellar recounts the scene at Streedagh Strand:

> On the fifth day, there came a great tempest which took us on the quarter, with a sea running as high as the Heaven, so that neither could our hawsers stand the strain nor could the sails be of any service. The ships were driven ashore on a beach of fine sand, and in the space of an hour the three vessels went to pieces. Of their crews, not more than 300 escaped, while more than 1,000 were drowned, among them many noblemen, chief officers, gentlemen and other persons and all their suites.

La Juliana, La Lavia and the *Santa Maria de Visōn* were all from the Levant Squadron of merchant ships, commanded by Martin de Bertendona. The galleon *San Juan,* of the Castilian Squadron, was also wrecked off Streedagh Strand, but not before Recalde had managed to save some of her guns and crew, who were put on board other ships.

The catalogue of misery continued. The *Falcon Blanco Mediano,* one of the Squadron of Hulks, sank off the coast of Galway. For a time her 100 crew were protected by the O'Flahertys of Connemara, but under threat from Sir Richard Bingham, Governor of Connaught, they were taken to Galway town. All were executed with the exception of the captain, who was held for ransom. Six young Dutchmen who had been forced to sail with the ship were at first pardoned by Bingham, but were later hanged on the express orders of the Lord Deputy Sir William Fitzwilliam in an act of gratuitous cruelty. Fitzwilliam was determined to exterminate any trace of opposition to English rule.

Sir George Carew was the Master of Ordnance in Dublin Castle. In a letter written on 28 September 1588 to Lord Walsyngham, he gave estimates of the Spanish losses as follows: sixteen ships lost, 6,000–7,000 Spanish drowned or killed and 1,100 executed. These figures do not include those who died on the return journey to Spain or shortly after they arrived home, including such notable leaders as Recalde and Don Miguel de Oquendo, commander of the Guipuzcoa Squadron.

Among the tales of great cruelty and greed against the Spanish survivors, there were heartening glimmers of humanity. Some of the local Irish chiefs were fiercely opposed to the English presence in Ireland and were eager to support her foes. They harboured the Spanish survivors at great personal risk. Sir Richard Bingham had issued a

View of Dunluce Castle, County Antrim, by the artist J. Nixon, first published in 1780. The castle belonged to Sorley Boy MacDonnell, an Irish chief who helped many Armada survivors to escape to Scotland. The *Girona* wreck-site is southeast of the cliff edge.

proclamation that anyone harbouring a Spaniard for more than twenty-four hours would be proclaimed a traitor, and would be hung, drawn and quartered. Sir Brian O'Rourke, Lord of Leitrim, gave shelter to 1,000 Spaniards and was consequently driven from Ireland by Bingham. He fled to Scotland, but was handed over to Elizabeth by James VI, son of Mary, Queen of Scots, who thought it prudent at the time to humour her. O'Rourke was executed in London in November 1591. Sorley Boy MacDonnell of Dunluce Castle on the North Antrim coast was another notable supporter of the endangered Spanish. He enabled survivors from *La Trinidad Valencera,* the *Girona* and some other ships to escape to his kinsfolk in Scotland.

Not all of the refugees from the Armada returned home. It is reported that some remained in Scotland as servants rather than return to Spain and serve in the wars against the Dutch. Some Armada survivors stayed with Hugh O'Neill, earl of Tyrone, and helped him in his conflict with Elizabeth. Pedro Blanco, one of the survivors of the wreck of the *Juliana* on Streedagh Strand, remained to become O'Neill's personal bodyguard. When O'Neill fled to Rome in 1607, Blanco accompanied him. Before he died, O'Neill wrote to Philip requesting that Blanco should be rewarded for his loyal service both to him and to the Spanish Crown, but there is no record that this was done.

THE EXTRAORDINARY TALE OF FRANCISCO DE CUELLAR

Captain Francisco de Cuellar was one of the Armada escapees whose tale of survival is truly inspirational. After many misfortunes and extraordinary adventures, he managed to reach Antwerp, from where he wrote a letter to Philip II, on 4 October 1589, recounting his travails in Ireland.

De Cuellar was obviously a man of exceptional bravery and great charm. He had been relieved of command of his ship, the *San Pedro,* because he had broken the fighting formation decreed beforehand and had sailed ahead of the fleet flagship. He was more fortunate than Captain Avila, however, and narrowly escaped hanging by defending himself with great spirit against the charge and winning the support of the Judge Advocate, Martin de Aranda. His life was spared but he was placed under arrest on board *La Lavia,* which was under Aranda's command. This ship was wrecked on

Streedagh Strand. De Cuellar (who could not swim), and Aranda attempted to float to shore on a hatch cover, but both were swept off by the rough seas. De Cuellar managed to scramble back on again, but Aranda, weighed down by the gold coins sewn into his doublet and hose, was lost.

De Cuellar's letter to Philip describes his first experience on Irish soil after his harrowing escape from the Atlantic:

> I believe that your Majesty will be surprised at seeing this letter on account of the little certainty which you could have had that I was alive, and I write that your Majesty may be sure of that, and somewhat at length ... I have not done so until now that God has brought me to this land of Flanders, whither I came maybe twelve days ago in company with the Spaniards who escaped from the ships that were wrecked off Ireland, Scotland and Shetland. There were more than twenty of them, the largest in the fleet, and on board was much of the choicest infantry, captains, ancients, colonels and other officers, also many gentlemen and persons of quality; and out of them all – and there were more than two hundred – not five escaped all told.

Thrown up on the sands, injured, cold and weak, he lay helplessly watching the savages, as he called the Irish, systematically robbing and stripping the dead and dying:

> ... the shore [was] lined with enemies who were dancing and jumping around with joy at the sight of our misfortune, and when anyone of our people reached the shore, down on him they came and at once stripped him of every stitch he had on him and then ill-treated him and left him covered with wounds.

By great good fortune he was not killed, but experienced many terrible vicissitudes. The day after the shipwreck, he resolved to find a safe place where he could plan his next move:

> At the dawn of day I began to walk, little by little, searching for a monastery of monks, that I might repair to it as best I could, which I arrived at with much trouble and toil. I found it deserted, and the church and images of the saints burned and completely ruined, and twelve Spaniards hanging within the church by the act of the Lutheran English, who went about searching for us to make an end of all of us who had escaped from the perils of the sea.

But he did at last reach a place of safety. De Cuellar was given succour by O'Rourke of Leitrim, and he speaks highly of him. Throughout his tribulations, de Cuellar retained his sense of humour. When he was living with O'Rourke, he mentions that the Irish chief's wife was exceedingly comely. One day he was sitting in the sun, chatting with her and some of her relatives and they asked him to read their palms. 'I rendered thanks to God, for now that I was become a gipsy among savages, there was nothing further to befall me ... I began to look at the hands of each, and to say to them a hundred thousand absurdities.' His 'fortune-telling' was so successful that hordes came to have their fortune told and O'Rourke had to intervene so that he was left in peace.

Although de Cuellar called the Irish savages, he was also fair in describing their better features.

> These savages liked us very much for they knew that we

were great enemies to the heretics and had come against them, and had it not been for them not one of us would now be alive. We were very grateful to them for this, although they were the first to rob and plunder those of us who reached the land alive.

De Cuellar could see what poor and wretched lives many of the ordinary Irish endured.

The nature of these savages is to live like beasts among the mountains ... They live in huts made of straw ... They eat but one meal a day, and that at night, and their ordinary food is oaten bread and butter...They sleep on the ground, upon rushes freshly cut and full of water or else frozen stiff. Most of the women are very pretty but ill dressed.

His stay with O'Rourke was probably the pleasantest episode throughout his long enforced sojourn in Ireland. His next lucky break was to be sheltered by MacClancy of Rosclogher Castle, County Leitrim, who was in constant conflict with the English. MacClancy's castle was built on a deep lake, it was surrounded by water and the only land access was via a deep marsh, so it was safe from attack. De Cuellar described it thus:

It was very strong and belonged to a savage gentleman, a very brave soldier and great enemy of the Queen of England and of her affairs, a man who had never cared to obey her or pay tribute, attending only to his castle and mountains, which made it strong.

Even so, hearing that the dreaded English were sending a great force against him, MacClancy took to the hills with his family and cattle.

Unwilling to accompany him, de Cuellar and eight of his companions undertook to defend the castle against the invaders. Left with food and plentiful supplies of ammunition and weapons, they withstood a siege of seventeen days. The weather became so bad, with heavy storms and much snow, that the English besiegers were forced to admit defeat and retreat to Dublin. By this time, de Cuellar says in his letter, the brave Spaniard and his companions were well-known throughout Ireland and their stand against the English was widely admired. MacClancy was so delighted with de Cuellar's defence of the castle that he gave the Spaniards many presents and offered de Cuellar his sister's hand in marriage. But de Cuellar was anxious to return home and politely declined the offer. However, one of MacClancy's sons told him that his father would keep the Spaniards safe and hidden there until Philip sent soldiers to rescue them.

> He [MacClancy] did not wish to give me permission to leave, nor to any Spaniard of those who were with him, saying that the roads were not safe; but his sole object was to detain us, that we might act as his guard.

Ten days after Christmas 1588, de Cuellar set off secretly with four soldiers to reach the North Antrim coast, where he believed a boat would be waiting to take them to Scotland – their transport had been vouched for by O'Cahan of Castleroe. They arrived at the coast after travelling twenty days, but the hoped-for boat from O'Cahan had already gone. On the Antrim coast he was given news of the fate of the *Girona,* and confirmed that Don Alonso de Leiva had been among the dead. Forced to remain in a village in Antrim until alternative transport could be arranged, de Cuellar occupied himself in his inimitable, debonair fashion: '... there were some very beautiful girls, with whom I was friendly, and went into their houses occasionally for society and conversation.'

Eventually, aided by the Bishop of Derry, Redmond Gallagher, de Cuellar and his companions reached Scotland and from there, Flanders. But even his arrival near Dunkirk was surrounded with drama. Four small boats had set out from Scotland, but only two managed to reach shore through the bombardment from the Dutch. Thrown out of his boat, de Cuellar managed to stagger ashore, dressed only in his shirt. From the shore, he and his companions were forced to watch the Dutch kill 270 Spaniards, leaving only three alive. However, de Cuellar was able to end his letter to the king by relating with some satisfaction that more than 400 Dutchmen had since been captured and had their heads chopped off. No quarter was given in sixteenth-century warfare.

PART FIVE

The Twentieth Century:
Excavating the Armada

LOCATING THE WRECK-SITES

Although the Armada losses were a matter of historical record and folklore for almost 400 years, it was not until the twentieth century that sustained efforts were made to salvage any of the shipwrecks. In his letter to King Philip, de Cuellar had confirmed that 'More than twenty [ships] were lost in the Kingdom of Ireland, with all the chivalry and flower of the Armada'.

The first dramatic discovery was made by the Belgian underwater archaeologist Robert Sténuit in 1967. The galleass *Girona* had been wrecked at Lacada Point, near the Giant's Causeway in County Antrim, on the morning of 26 October 1588. Sténuit's excavation of the wreck was to electrify the diving world and spark the world's interest in maritime archaeology, which was really in its infancy. The many secrets and treasures of the underwater world were awaiting discovery, recovery and display for the education and delight of all. The fortunate result of Sténuit's efforts is that the Ulster Museum now owns the excavated objects from

Robert Sténuit, counting the gold and silver coins recovered from the *Girona*.

three Armada ships – the *Girona*, *La Trinidad Valencera* and the *Santa Maria de la Rosa* – making it the repository of a very large percentage of sixteenth-century Spanish artefacts.

In 1971 the City of Derry Sub-Aqua Club discovered the wreck-site of *La Trinidad Valencera* in Kinnagoe Bay, County Donegal, and finds from that ship, brought up under the direction of Dr Colin Martin over the next two years, gave a great insight into the world of the sixteenth-century mariner and soldier. *La Trinidad Valencera*, a refurbished Venetian merchant ship and one of the largest in the fleet, had run aground and broken up in Kinnagoe Bay on 16 September 1588.

In 1978, the remains of the *Santa Maria de la Rosa* were located in Blasket Sound, County Kerry, after a painstaking search that had lasted five years. The *Santa Maria de la Rosa*, the vice-flagship of the Guipuzcoa Squadron, was wrecked in Blasket Sound on 21 September 1588.

Three ships located off Streedagh Strand, County Sligo,

the *Juliana*, *La Lavia* and the *Santa Maria de Visōn*, await excavation.

THE STORY OF THE GIRONA

Robert Sténuit had spent many years consulting Spanish and English archive documents concerning the whereabouts of the Spanish wreck. In the end, local knowledge of the wreck-site – the area the wreck was eventually found in, off Lacada Point, is called Port na Spaniagh by locals – was to prove correct. Sténuit found the first sign of the *Girona* – a large boat-shaped lead ingot – at a depth of thirty feet , and the story of the fate of the ship gradually emerged from beneath the waves at Lacada Point.

> ... I had found the wreck. I closed my eyes, and felt my mouth, frozen with cold, turn up into a smile. The elation I felt was calm, a slow but very deep joy, a feeling of relief almost.

The *Girona* was a large galleass that had been built at Naples, which, at that time, was under Spanish rule. She was one of four vessels of this type, under the command of Don Hugo de Moncado, comprising the Squadron of the Kingdom of Naples. Her captain was Fabricio Spinola of Genoa.

We know that the *Girona* carried a complement of fifty cannon, forty-five pieces of which had been jettisoned to make room for extra crew and soldiers before she left Killybegs harbour in County Donegal. She had sheltered to make repairs to her rudder and sails. She carried a total crew of 500, made up of 121 officers and men, the remainder being the

This map shows the named Armada wreck-sites around the coast of Ireland.

oarsmen. In addition to the cannon, she carried 8,000 pieces of iron and stone shot. The foodstuffs she carried were as follows: 750 portions of hard tack, 100 casks of wine, 62cwt of lard, 62cwt of cheese, 60 casks of tuna fish, 40 casks of sardines, 15cwt of rice, dried beans and pulses, as well as raisins, oil, vinegar, sugar, salt and semolina. (One hundred weight is equal to 112 kilograms.) We know all these facts from the lists kept in the Simancas Archives in the Public Record Office in Valladolid, Spain.

As the *Girona* sheltered and made repairs in Killybegs harbour, news of her whereabouts had reached the survivors of two other ships, the *Duquessa Santa Ana*, which had run aground at Loughros Mor Bay, County Donegal, and the *Santa Maria Encoronada*, which had been wrecked in Blacksod Bay, County Mayo. The leader of the two groups of survivors was Don Alonso Martinez de Leiva, once again demonstrating his resourcefulness and stamina. His ship, the carrack *La Rata Encoronada*, had been in constant pursuit and attack from the English fleet. When the orders to return to Spain were given, his ship had been blown off course towards the west coast of Ireland. Attempting to seek shelter in Blacksod Bay, the ship ran aground. De Leiva disembarked his crew, taking all useful equipment with them, and then set fire to the ship so that it would not be of any use to the enemy. He marched his men to a small castle at Doona, but when he heard that the *Duquessa Santa Ana* was nearby in Elly Bay, on the far side of Blacksod Bay, he made his way there, got his men on board and set sail.

They had sailed as far north as Loughros Mor Bay when

DE LEIVA'S BRAVERY

De Leiva's injuries after his second shipwreck are described by James Machary, who was left behind when the *Girona* sailed from Killybegs: 'Don Alonso before he came to land was hurt in the leg by the capstan of the ship in such sort as he was neither able to go nor ride, neither during the 9 days of his encampment, nor upon his removal, but was carried from that place to the place wherein the galleass (named *Girona*) lay, between 4 men, being 19 miles distant, where likewise he and all his company encamped 12 to 14 days in which time the galleass was finished, and made ready for the sea as well as she could be.'

the ship was wrecked. Managing again to disembark his crew safely, de Leiva occupied another small castle on an island in Kiltoorish Lake, County Donegal. There he received news that the *Girona* had reached the harbour of Killybegs to make repairs. Although one leg had been badly injured by a capstan (the cylinder used for winding anchor cable) during the second shipwreck and he was confined to a litter, he led his men the nineteen miles to Killybegs, where he organised the *Girona*'s repairs.

In order to accommodate 1,300 men on board a ship designed to carry 500, he ordered all but five of her defensive cannon to be jettisoned. As the galleass attempted to sail north to southwest Scotland, it was caught yet again in the terrible autumn storms, and with its rudder damaged beyond repair it drifted helplessly on to the rocks at Lacada Point on the morning of 26 October 1588. All on board were lost, except for five survivors. Over 400 years later, de Leiva's Cross of a Knight of Santiago was

This simple gold cross, inlaid with enamel and with the arms terminating in *fleur-de-lys*, was the Cross of a Knight of Santiago, one of the most prestigious Orders of Chivalry. Its noble owner was Don Alonso Martinez de Leiva, commander designate of the Armada, who was shipwrecked twice before he was lost with the *Girona*.

recovered from the seabed, confirming de Cuellar's narrative that this brave captain had been lost with the *Girona*.

A few days before the dive that would see the first evidence of the *Girona* since that fateful night in 1588, Robert Sténuit went to Port na Spaniagh to view the area where he hoped the wreck lay waiting. His description of this wild part of the Antrim coast is eerily evocative:

> ... Port na Spaniagh is out of this world. An amphitheatre of 400 ft high cliffs, sheer and terrifying. The wind howled round our ears ... The rock was black – the cliffs were black, with gashes of red where men have cut out paths ... Mounds of fallen debris were piled up at the bottom to form a chaotic mass of boulders where the beach ought to have been. All the floating wrecks from miles around end up here ... The wildness of the place made a deep impression on me. It's a place that calls for death, cries out for tragedy. It's too much. A film set. Nature has overdone it. I could see the great ship being pounded to pieces down there by the waves that never stop. Her sides crack, and men are thrown out onto the black rocks, snatched up by the breakers, hurled down again, smashed, broken up like old puppets.

During the underwater excavations of the *Girona* wreck-site, which commenced in 1968 and continued until 1969, a dazzling amount of treasure was recovered in the form of Renaissance jewellery and coins. The reason for its presence was that the officers of the Armada had been chosen from the noblest and wealthiest houses in Spain. The *Girona* also had on board the officers from two other ships, and we know that many young nobles had followed Don Alonso de Leiva to death or glory. These officers carried some of their personal fortunes with them in coinage. James Machary, an Irishman who had been conscripted in Lisbon to join the Armada, attested to this. He had the good fortune to be left behind when the *Girona* sailed from Killybegs. When he was subsequently interrogated by Lord Deputy Fitzwilliam, he said that after de Leiva was shipwrecked for the first time from *La Rata Encoronada*, and he and the other men were taken on board the *Santa Ana*, they took with them 'all the goods they had in the shipp of any valewe, as plate, apparell, monie, jewells, weapons, armor etc.'

Several religious medals, given to all crew members before departure, were found at the wreck-site. A heavy gold cross, one of silver, one of bronze and one of lead, as well as a small bronze gilt figure of the crucified Christ, were all recovered in the excavation, showing that each man carried religious symbols appropriate to his rank.

A heavy gold ring with flattened bezel bearing the initials 'IHS' was also found. These initials are an abbreviation of the Greek for 'Jesus' and are the sacred monogram of the Jesuit order, founded by St Ignatius Loyola, who died in 1556. The ring undoubtedly belonged to one of the Jesuit priests who accompanied the fleet; it is

This gold ring with the initials IHS – a sacred monogram – is likely to have belonged to a Jesuit priest accompanying the *Girona*.

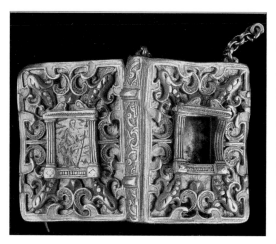

A reliquary is a receptacle for holy relics. This gold reliquary is in the form of a book, with a depiction of St John the Baptist on the cover (left). *Girona.*

reported that the Armada set sail with 200 clerics on board. An Agnus Dei reliquary in the form of a little golden book has a depiction of St John the Baptist on the cover. It consists of five circular compartments, which would have contained wax tablets bearing the image of Agnus Dei, made from the wax of Paschal (Passover) candles that were blessed by Pope Sixtus V.

Another religious artefact was a silver gilt lid with a large 'A' contained in a circle on top, which was part of an altar cruet set. The 'A' signified *agua* – this lid would have been a cover for the water vessel commonly seen on altar tops, accompanied by a vessel to contain wine.

Top of silver gilt altar cruet recovered from the *Girona*. The 'A' is for *agua* (water).

Several Orders of Chivalry were found and we know that the Cross of a Knight of Santiago de Compostela belonged to de Leiva. The Order of Santiago and the Order of Chivalry of

Alcantara were originally founded as religious military orders whose purpose was to fight the invading Moors in Spain. The Cross of a Knight of Alcantara cannot be attributed to a particular Spanish nobleman. Neither can the Cross of a Knight of St John of Jerusalem, also found at the wreck site, although attempts were made to attribute it to the *Girona*'s captain, Fabricio Spinola.

The Order of Alcantara was established about 1156, near a hermitage dedicated to St Julian that was surrounded by wild pear trees. Its members were first called Knights of St Julian of the Pear Tree, but when the Knights defended Alcantara against the Moors, they adopted the name of that city. The Order of Alcantara is a small lidded container with an engraving of St Julian and the pear tree on one side, and on the other an open-work cross with each terminal ending in a *fleur-de-lys* – the symbol of the Order. *Girona.*

One of the most famous finds made by Sténuit was a magnificent set of eleven lapis lazuli cameos, set in gold mounts and decorated with pearls and green enamel (the twelfth and final cameo was found later by another diver). These would have formed a grand chain, as seen in contemporary portraits. The cameos depicted twelve Roman Caesars. Unfortunately, not all the lapis lazuli settings survived, but of the surviving seven, two have been identified from images on coins as Domitian (AD51–AD96) and Trajan (AD53–AD117). These two cameos retained their full complement of eight pearls, four on each side, and some traces of green enamel.

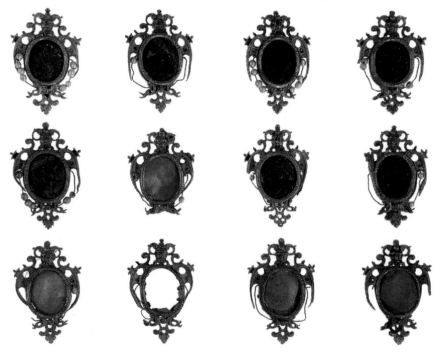

Twelve portrait cameos of Byzantine Caesars in lapis lazuli, gold, enamel and pearls were recovered from the *Girona*. These would have formed a large chain, familiar from sixteenth-century portraits of Spanish grandees. Two of the most complete cameos still retain some of their green enamel and four pearls on each side. The pearls could have come from the oyster beds at Venezuela, traded by Indian pearl-divers to the Spanish conquerors.

The pearls would have come from the oyster beds at Venezuela, and would have been traded by the South American pearl-divers with their Spanish conquerors. The lapis lazuli gemstones probably came from Afghanistan in southern Asia.

Twelve gold cameo mounts were recovered, minus their settings, and only two portions survived of what had been a magnificent gold chain set with two pearls and a ruby. Portions of another composite gold chain were recovered in a damaged state. There are fragments of four other gold chains and several half portions of jewel settings. One complete and one half delicate gold filigree mount doubtless adorned the garments of a Spanish grandee. Thirty-three crushed gold buttons were further evidence of the rich and elaborate clothing worn by the Armada leaders. One of the most surprising survivals, because it is so tiny, is a minute gold rosette, which may have formed the eyelet of a lace tie. Apart from the buttons and the gold rosettes, the only other finds connected with clothing were two bronze buckles and the leather soles of seven shoes.

The most appealing jewel from the *Girona* treasure is the gold and ruby salamander pendant. This pendant encapsulates so much of the Spanish Empire at that time, it has become an icon for the Armada. The importance of gold and silver from the American colonies in sustaining the Spanish Empire cannot be emphasised too strongly. This jewel, in the form of an exotic animal – either a real Mexican salamander or a mythical creature – reflects the huge importance of the colonies. The native craftsmen were sublime goldsmiths and many of their ideas were borrowed by their conquerors. Although a vast number of native ornaments were melted down for their gold content, many others were preserved for the enjoyment of the Spanish nobility. Hernan Cortes, the conqueror of Mexico, recorded in 1526 that among the gold ornaments sent to Spain for Charles V, Philip's father, was a 'winged lizard' or salamander. In legend, the salamander was meant to have the magical properties of being able to extinguish and to survive fire. This would have made it a potent good-luck charm on board a wooden fighting ship, where fire was one of the greatest hazards.

The salamander appears again on the bezel of a fine gold ring from the *Girona* site. Here it is flanked on both sides by a human head. Heads were frequently depicted by pre-Hispanic South American goldsmiths on breast, nose and ear ornaments.

In all, twelve gold rings were recovered and although most had lost their jewelled settings, one still retained two cut diamonds. The personal and sentimental nature of some of the jewellery is revealed by two gold rings in particular – the Madame de Champagney ring and the *No Tengo* ring. The *No Tengo* ring is a particularly

A small gold ring – one terminal shows a hand holding a heart, the other shows a buckle. The poignant Spanish inscription reads: *No tengo mas que dar te* – I have nothing more to give thee. It underlines the great human tragedy of so many loved ones lost with the Armada.

touching memento. No one knows the identity of its owner, but it bears the inscription: *No tengo mas que dar te* – I have nothing more to give you.

Madame de Champagney's ring was being worn as a family heirloom by her grandson, Don Tomas Perrenoto. He died with the wreck of the *Girona* at the age of twenty-two. This ring posed something of a problem because of the date, 1524, inscribed on it, but painstaking work by Robert Sténuit unravelled the mystery. Madame de Champagney, the grandmother of Don Thomas, was Nicole Bonvalot of Besancon. Her husband, Nicolas, inherited the lands of Champagney from his brother, Jerome, who had in turn inherited the land from his father, Frederick Perrenot. It is supposed that the ring was worn in her honour by Frederick, on the birth of her second son, Jerome, in 1524; she had eleven children in all. When

Some of the jewellery found on the *Girona* can be connected with members of the ship's company. This gold ring originally belonged to Madame de Champagney. She had given it to her twenty-one-year-old grandson, Don Tomas Perrenoto, who perished with the ship.

Nicolas inherited the land from Jerome, he apparently received the ring bearing his grandmother's name as well.

These personal mementoes underline the great and tragic loss to Spain of almost 1,300 men who perished with the *Girona*. They also evoke the futility, waste and cruelty of warfare.

Hundreds of gold and silver coins were recovered at the *Girona* site, and they again show the close connection between medieval Spanish wealth, Spain's conquests in the New World and the extent of her empire in the sixteenth century. The 414 gold coins, 789 silver coins and 122 copper coins had been minted in six different countries: Spain, Portugal, the Kingdom of the Two Sicilies, the Republic of Genoa, Mexico and Peru. Although the Spanish had established mints at Mexico, Lima, in Peru, and Potosi, in Bolivia, almost eighty-five percent of the gold coins had been minted at Seville. Situated at the head of the great Guadalquivir River, Seville was the centre for gold coming from the New World.

The silver coins were made from silver mined at Potosi. Silver flowed from the mine at Potosi and provided one of the financial mainstays of the empire. Only a few of the coins recovered come from the Spanish mints at Mexico, Lima and Potosi, because at this date coin production was just starting to develop in the colonies.

The sixteenth-century coins are rare and important. Silver eight-real pieces from the Lima mint bear the mark of the assayer, Diego de la Torre. The function of the assayer was to ensure that the coins were all of sufficient weight and precious metal content. Eight-real pieces from the Mexico mint are also represented in the collection, but the largest proportion of both gold and silver coins came from the Seville mint. Another important coin is a silver testone bearing the inscription: *Philip R Ang B PRI HI* (Philip as King of England, 1554–1556), which was minted at Naples, reminding us again that he had once been the husband of an English Queen. A gold Portuguese San Vincente from the Lisbon mint of John III (1521–1557) is a further reminder of a very important part of Spain's Empire.

Coins recovered from the *Girona*.

In confirmation of the elegance of the table settings and the incongruous courtly behaviour of the ship's officers on board a warship, four silver candlesticks, minus their bases, were recovered, as well as two silver tapersticks. Over forty handles and tines of silver forks were also recovered. The fork handles were in the shape of mens' torsos, clubs and cloven hooves. Laurence Flanagan, writing in 1998, says that in the fifteenth and early sixteenth centuries, forks were regarded with dismay by the Church, who thought them fit to be used only by prostitutes. However, towards the end of the sixteenth century forks had obviously found favour at Philip's religious court. The depiction of cloven hooves on fork handles echoes their previous devilish and sinful connection. Many years after the original excavation, the most complete and modern-looking silver fork was recovered at the *Girona* site by a member of Portrush Sub-Aqua Club. It had four tines and the initials 'SM' on top of the handle. So far these initials have not been connected with a particular noble member of the ship's company, but such personalised cutlery obviously belonged to someone of importance.

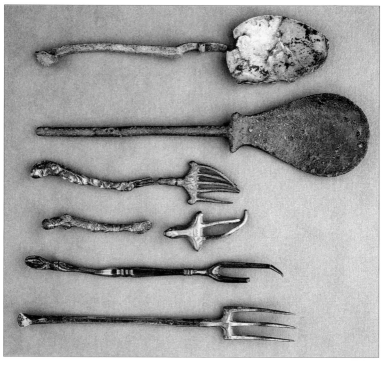

The silver spoon and forks all come from the *Girona*; the pewter spoon from *La Trinidad Valencera*. The *Girona* forks had two, three, four or five tines and the handles terminated in cloven hooves, mens' torsos or clubs. The odd one out is the modern-looking fork (bottom) with three tines and the initials 'SM' on the top. Its owner has not yet been identified.

Perhaps less numerically and visually impressive, but no less interesting than the silver coins which were found, were the silver objects that survived in an easily recognisable form. Hundreds of very small fragments of silver and silver gilt dishes, silver wire and small silver finials were recovered. Although we know that by 1370 silver was being marked at Barcelona to indicate its precious metal content, there was no regulation by law to mark all Spanish silver. As a result, there are no silversmiths' marks on any of the surviving silver pieces.

Two fragments of highly decorated silver plates and a simple scroll handle demonstrate several styles of sixteenth-century Spanish tableware. The hundreds of small fragments of silver and silver gilt dishes recovered indicate that there must have been many dozens of these on board. An ornate silver jug spout sculpted with the mask of Bacchus, the god of wine, probably came from a wine jug. One ornate silver gilt spout and a plain spout of sheet silver were also found, but no trace of the vessels to which they belonged.

Silver was not just used for coins and dishes. A silver bosun's whistle in three fragments was found and several pieces of silver sword guards. Bosun's whistles had been in use since the thirteenth century for signalling. These silver whistles would have belonged to junior officers and were used for conveying commands throughout the boat. Gold whistles were worn as a badge of rank by senior officers in the Spanish fleet.

Three portions of a silver bosun's whistle from the *Girona*. These were used by junior officers for signalling throughout the ship.

One of the most attractive silverware objects is a small dolphin mount. The dolphin was a popular seafaring decoration and five bronze gilt dolphin mounts were found as well as a gold ear- and toothpick in the form of a dolphin.

Although the noble commanders dressed and dined in as much luxury as possible, the recovery of the top portions of eight small silver perfume bottles, one crystal dropper and many body fragments of other bottles remind us of the stinking conditions which existed below decks in a wooden fighting ship.

Silver perfume flask and crystal dropper from the *Girona*.

The ordinary soldier and infantryman had less elegant, but no less functional, wooden spoons and metal knives with wooden handles decorated with metal studs. Instead of silver gilt dishes they had wooden plates and bowls and pottery containers of many sorts. Only a few pottery sherds were found at the *Girona* site, but lots of wooden plates and dishes were recovered from the wreck-site of *La Trinidad Valencera*.

ARMAMENTS AND OTHER FINDS FROM THE *GIRONA*

In case it should be thought that only objects of precious metals were found at the *Girona* site, there were many other finds of equal interest if not monetary worth: six pairs of bent bronze navigational dividers; one bronze astrolabe and a second in fragments; twenty copper pot handles; copper nails; lead seals for jars; the trigger guard of a musket; the top portions of two small silver keys; wooden portions of muskets and a small bronze gilt disc. All of these finds provide important information about life in sixteenth-century Spain and life on board ship.

The bronze gilt disc was much corroded by sea water, but sufficient numbers and letters are visible to conjecture that this was part of a more sophisticated navigational aid, probably an astronomical compendium. Apart from the navigational dividers, the astrolabes and this metal disc, the only other navigational aids discovered were two sounding leads.

Some of the most intriguing objects recovered from the *Girona* site were beads. Two were giant, agate, egg-shaped beads, heavily water rolled. Another two were a portion of a bloodstone bead and a portion of a jade bead and there was

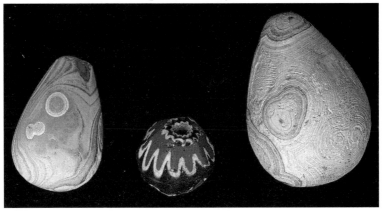

Two large agate beads, heavily water-rolled, which were recovered from the *Girona*. They may have belonged to an unfortunate man from one of the Spanish colonies, enslaved with his companions as a rower on the galleass. The smaller, multicoloured bead was made at Murano in Venice. *La Trinidad Valencera*.

one small, plain, round wooden bead. The stones used to make all four beads are common to Middle and South America, but not to Europe. It can only be supposed that these beads were the property of Native American slaves, chained to their oars in the galleass. Although not all the oarsmen were from the colonies, some were convicts and captives from other Spanish conflicts. At that time, captured enemy sailors were often sent to the galleys if they were not executed outright.

Of the original armaments which were on board when the

The arms of Philip II as King of England, from the large siege gun recovered from *La Trinidad Valencera*.

Girona sailed from La Coruña, only two complete cannon and one mouthpiece of a cannon were recovered. A breech-loading bronze esmeril still has the arms of Spain and the chain of the Order of the Golden Fleece visible on the barrel, despite hundreds of years of sea action. The esmeril was a small gun designed to be mounted on a swivel spike, on the side of the ship, for quick aim at enemy personnel. In the sixteenth century, large cannon were loaded with the powder charge from the muzzle-end. Small cannon, such as the esmeril, had their charge of powder in a detachable powder chamber

Bronze, breech-loading, lightweight swivel gun or esmeril, used for rapid shipboard firing, accompanied by breech-blocks and cannon balls. *Girona*.

or breech-block, which was inserted into the breech-end of the gun. This made rapid reloading much easier. The bronze breech-block was found in position in the esmeril, with its charge of gunpowder still intact.

In all, fourteen bronze breech blocks were found to fit various sizes of breech-loading guns. The other complete cannon found was a bronze half-saker. The name 'saker' referred to a bird – the sacred falcon – and a half-saker was a half-size cannon. The half-saker had the remains of its lifting dolphins above the trunnions. (The lifting dolphins were two metal mounts in the shape of dolphins, through which ropes or cable could be threaded to move them around; the trunnions

Ordnance recovered from the *Girona*.

were projecting pieces on which the cannon rested when it was mounted on a gun carriage.) It also had the faint remains of the arms of Spain on the upper part of the long gun barrel. The damaged muzzle portion of a breech-loading gun was the only other large cannon found, and we are reminded of de Leiva's order to jettison the heavy armaments to lighten the ship's load.

Smaller arms were represented by the complete wooden stock of an arquebus with its ramrod and lead ball still in the chamber, five dagger hilts, one leather dagger sheath, several sword guards, hundreds of lead shot

A wooden arquebus stock with its wooden ramrod and several lead balls. *Girona*.

for both muskets and arquebuses and many stone and iron cannon balls to fit cannon of various sizes.

One of the greatest problems on long sea voyages was carrying sufficient nourishing food for those on board. Much of the food carried by the Armada ships went bad and this caused great sickness for the unfortunate crews. The spoiling of the food was partly caused by packing it in barrels which had been made from unseasoned wood because of the haste of departure of the grand fleet. Unseasoned wood has not lost its moisture content, so its dampness causes dried food to rot. Fishing was one way of obtaining fresh food, and the finding of five lead fishing weights indicates that sixteenth-century mariners had some understanding that fresh food was necessary for healthy crews.

Heavy, boat-shaped lead ingots were carried on board the Armada ships for making lead shot for muskets and arquebuses.

In all, twenty-seven complete and one half large lead ingots were recovered. There were also sixty-two flat, roughly rectangular lead ingots, which had been perforated with various round, square and star-shaped holes. The lead ingots were used to make musket and arquebus shot, and as sheeting for hull repairs. A roll of thin, flattened lead sheet was also found at the wreck-site, presumably ready for nailing across any leaking seams in the ship's timbers.

None of the ship's timbers survived the pounding of the Atlantic Ocean, but a great number of bronze coaks did withstand the erosive effects of their environment. Coaks are square bronze bearings with a central hole, which were inserted in the wooden pulley blocks. The heavy rigging ropes for the sails were threaded through these and this prevented the wood splitting when the ropes were continually hauled up and down. Other remnants of the ship's rigging were a few heavily corroded iron shackles. Only one, heavily corroded, iron anchor was found of the *Girona*'s original complement of four.

Square bronze coak set (above) and wooden pulley block (below). The coak prevented the wood from splitting when the heavy sail ropes were pulled through it.

Many of the smaller finds are of equal interest. Two lead bale seals, which were used to close the bindings on supply containers of cloth or wood, were recovered from the seabed. One has the Portuguese coat of arms on one side and a representation of the world on the other. Once Portugal had been the paramount European power with an extensive empire throughout the world, now, with its defeat by the Spanish, it was Spain's turn.

FINDS FROM *LA TRINIDAD VALENCERA*

The forty-two gun, 1,100-tonne merchant ship *La Trinidad Valencera* was badly damaged by heavy seas on 12 September 1588. She took in so much water her pumps could not cope and, seeking shelter, she ran aground on a reef in Kinnagoe Bay, at Malin Head in north Donegal. The fate of her crew has been related. Her remains were discovered in February 1971 by members of the City of Derry Sub-Aqua Club ,who were alerted to their find when they located one of her guns. Other guns were found and, anxious that the best and most scientific means of recovery should be employed, Dr Colin Martin, one of Britain's foremost nautical archaeologists, was requested to direct the excavations.

In many ways the finds from *La Trinidad Valencera* complemented those from the *Girona*. The combination of the finds from both ships augmented on a grand scale our knowledge about sixteenth-century life in general and life on board ship in particular. Because *La Trinidad Valencera* had foundered in a silty basin, a great deal of organic material was preserved. Many quite large pieces of ship's timbers, pulley blocks and an astonishing variety of wooden dishes, remains of barrels and pieces of what seem to be furniture were well-preserved under the silt.

ARMAMENTS AND OTHER FINDS FROM
LA TRINIDAD VALENCERA

A battery of great guns was recovered. It included three siege

Large, bronze, muzzle-loading siege gun, now mounted on a replica
gun carriage, one of three recovered from *La Trinidad Valencera*.
The breech end bears the arms of Philip II of Spain as King of England.
It was made by the Belgian gunsmith Remigy de Halut in 1556.

guns from the royal train of Philip II, made for him in Malines
in 1556 by the noted Belgian gunsmith Remigy de Halut, who
made guns for many European powers. Rare pieces of gunner's equipment provided invaluable information on load-
ing and firing a sixteenth-century cannon. These rare pieces
included three wooden shot gauges, pieces of a gunner's
rule, a copper powder scoop and stone, lead and iron shot of
different calibre. These finds provide a cross-section of the
equipment required on the gun-decks.

A wooden sponge head and a goatskin were also found.
The goatskin would have been dipped in water, wrapped
around the wooden sponge head and used for clearing the
burning debris out of the cannon barrel before a further gunpowder charge was inserted. Two copper buckets would

have been on hand to hold water for dipping the goatskin; copper gave off no sparks and so was ideal to use near gunpowder. A bronze touch-hole cover was recovered from one of the large cannon. A wooden linstock in the shape of a human hand and arm, and the head of another linstock in the shape of a dragon's head were two more rare pieces of gunnery equipment found. The linstock held the slow match that lit the charge of powder and fired the cannon.

In addition to massive siege cannon, the finds from the *Trinidad* demonstrated several types of unpleasant anti-personnel weapons in use. A ceramic fire pot was found – this would have been filled with flammable material and thrown among the vulnerable ship's sails. A long wooden tube filled with flammable material,

Copper bucket, wooden sponge head, copper scoop, wooden linstock, iron shot and three wooden shot gauges from *La Trinidad Valencera*. The copper bucket was for sluicing down the decks, the wooden sponge head was covered with goatskin and used to clean the inside of the gun barrels after firing, the copper scoop was for pouring in gunpowder, the linstock was used to hold the slow match to light the powder charge and the three shot gauges were used to measure the size of shot for a specific gun.

called a *bomba*, was another device that was hurled on to the enemy's ship. A third type of explosive device was made from metal fragments stuck around a central explosive charge, which would send shrapnel flying among the gun-deck's crews.

La Trinidad Valencera yielded a very important number of

organic items, the kind of items which had not survived at the *Girona* site. A portion of the huge rope anchor cable, wooden staves from both large and small barrels, wooden bungs from casks, wineskin stoppers and many other pieces of turned wood were found. A wooden comb with ordinary teeth on one side and very close-together teeth on the other is an unhappy reminder of the presence of lice on even the best-dressed man on board. A pair of wooden bellows would have been used to keep the galley fire going. A large cake of resin was probably used to make the sails waterproof, or perhaps to pour on the seams between the ship's planking. The ship's officers presumably whiled away part of the outward voyage with pleasant pastimes such as music and games because the fingerboard of a lute-like musical instrument and two wooden balls were also found. Fragments of a small wooden cage may have been for a little songbird.

THE TEREDO WORM

The teredo or ship worm, *Teredo navalis*, is a type of mollusc that causes tremendous damage to the underwater timbers of ships, piers and sea-dikes by boring its way into the wood. Early seafarers tried various means of protecting their ships. In the sixteenth century, the Portuguese and Spanish attempted to solve the problem by treating the timbers with a mixture of tallow, lime and sulphur or fish oil.

Other finds illuminate the lives of the ordinary sailor on board. Many wooden pulley blocks, bronze breech-blocks and several types of ship's hammer were found. Caulking hammers were essential in rendering the seams between wooden plank-built boards watertight. The Portuguese and the Spanish were particularly diligent in their attempts to protect the wooden timbers of underwater hulls from teredo worms, which were so damaging in tropical waters. One giant single pulley block from *La Trinidad Valencera* bears testament to the massive damage the teredo worm could cause.

A remarkable number of woollen and silk textile fragments survived the wreck and the subsequent centuries underwater. Among the 400 pieces found were a silk tassel, the golden velvet collar of a doublet, a woollen sock and many pieces of decorative red and yellow silk braid. Many shoe soles and upper parts of leather shoes were also recovered, very similar to those found at the *Girona* site.

The Spanish were quite prepared to pursue a military campaign on land once they had defeated the English navy. To underline their determination to lay waste any large cities which might have attempted resistance, two giant, iron-shod, wooden gun-carriage wheels, 152cm in diameter, were found. These were part of the dismantled sections of six gun carriages known to be on board *La Trinidad Valencera*, which were part of a siege train to carry the giant bronze cannon. Fragments of a campaign tent with six wooden toggles belonging to it were another proof that they anticipated land battles as well as sea battles in their conquest of England.

The *Trinidad*'s contents reveal more about the foodstuffs on board. The contents of an olive jar were discovered to be lentils. Three pine cones and a bay leaf provided further insight on the diet available. A plum stone from the *Girona* and a Brazil nut from the *Santa Maria de la Rosa* show that at least some effort was made to provide fresh food for the crews.

The Armada ships carried with them all the provisions for a long journey. Pottery vessels like these were called olive jars, but could contain wine, oil or even lentils. Most of the food on board was salted or dried. Fresh kernels of pine cones were eaten as a delicacy, and the remainder of the cone could be used as fuel for fires. *La Trinidad Valencera*.

A very wide range of damaged pewterware was salvaged from the ship. After much conservation work had been completed on these by the staff of the Ulster Museum's conservation laboratory, they emerged as fine goblets, large bowls, many plates and dishes of varying sizes, spoons, a jug and an interesting open-bodied container. This last item had a spout and a suspension ring and may have been used to feed invalids on board. The remains of a small, complete, pottery medicine jar and half of one very large pottery medicine jar show that shipboard sickness was a very real hazard on long journeys. The two bronze mortars and pestles found would have been used to grind up medicinal roots and leaves.

The pewterware dish with its spout and suspension ring (back right) may have been used for feeding sick members of the crew. *La Trinidad Valencera*.

The discovery of a large multi-coloured glass bead, made in the famous Venetian glass factory of Murano, confirms the fact that the *Trinidad* was a refurbished merchant ship. Such large glass beads are often found on sites in America, where the Spanish went as conquerors or colonisers. They took beads with them to trade with the natives, inevitably for much more valuable commodities such as gold. This bead, along with two bronze Venetian guns and a bronze and iron swivel gun, were probably part of her original cargo. In the sixteenth century, because of pirate raids, merchant ships carried their own armaments to protect their precious loads.

MEDICINES

Medicines which would have been carried on board include chinaroot, henna, sarsaparilla, mercury and guaiacum. Chinaroot was used for vomiting and sickness, especially seasickness. Henna flowers and leaves could be used both internally and externally for jaundice, leprosy, smallpox and infections of the skin. Sarsaparilla root was pounded up and used internally for pulmonary complaints, when used as a wash it was said to cure ulcers and shingles. The Spanish also believed that it cured syphilis. Mercury was commonly used to treat venereal diseases. Guaiacum bark was widely believed to cure syphilis in the sixteenth century and to be helpful for skin diseases and scrofula.

Venice was the most important trading centre of that era,
and luxury goods from many countries passed through its port on
their way to their eventual destination. A complete Ming bowl,
found on *La Trinidad Valencera*, is an example of the type
of exotic import procured for the Spanish court.

The finds from the *Trinidad* demonstrate the equipment
needed on board a fighting ship, both for its defence and for
the comfort of its crew. They also provide a wealth of information on how the nobles and the ordinary sailor and soldier
dressed and ate in the sixteenth century. Important information on navigational aids was provided in the shape of the top
and base of an hourglass, the wooden base of a compass and a
set of bronze navigational dividers in mint condition.

Only one copper coin was recovered from the *Trinidad*
wreck. It was a Portuguese five Reis of Sebastien I
(1557–1578). Unlike the *Girona*, all the personnel on board the
ship had already reached land by the time the ship had
broken up, and had therefore taken all their personal wealth
with them.

FINDS FROM THE *SANTA MARIA DE LA ROSA*

The third Armada ship to be excavated was the *Santa Maria de la Rosa*. It was a ship of 945 tonnes, carried 250 men and was armed with twenty-six guns. The *Santa Maria de la Rosa* was the vice-flagship of the Guipuzcoa Squadron, under the command of Don Miguel de Oquendo. She sank almost instantly in Blasket Sound, County Kerry, on 21 September 1588, before the horrified gaze of several other Armada ships who were also sheltering there.

Although the whereabouts of the wreck was known, preliminary searches from 1973 until 1976 failed to find her. Finally, a diving team led by Sidney Wignall, assisted by John Grattan and a team of service divers, found the first real clue in 1978: a large anchor, four metres long, was located along with three other anchors. The actual wreck lay about 200 yards to the southeast of the submerged Stromboli reef. The site was marked by a large ballast mount of stones, iron shot, lead musket balls and six large lead ingots similar to those found at the *Girona* site. The discovery of two pewter plates with the name Matute under the rim proved that this really was the wreck of the *Santa Maria de la Rosa*. Documentary sources confirmed that Francisco Ruiz Matute had been captain of infantry on board the ship.

Since the *Santa Maria de la Rosa* was a vice-flagship it was supposed that she might have had much treasure on board. De Aramburu, who wrote about her loss some years later, mentions that she was carrying a fortune in gold and plate.

However, none of it has ever been recovered. Finds included iron shot, timbers, iron nails, lead shot and ingots, pot sherds, a Brazil nut and pieces of animal and human bone, but no jewels or coins. Parts of the hull structure were preserved underneath the ballast mound. These remaining parts showed the hull to be of light construction, quite unsuited to the rough conditions experienced on an Atlantic voyage.

The finds from the *Santa Maria* had to be sold at auction to offset the high cost of recovering the objects from the seabed. The Ulster Museum was able to acquire the two Matute plates, a large damaged pewter plate, a small lightweight copper bowl, half an iron cannon ball and the Brazil nut.

The customised plate of Captain Francisco Ruiz Matute,
captain of the guard on the *Santa Maria de la Rosa*.

Aftermath:
the sixteenth century and beyond

Flavit et dissipati sunt

The immediate aftermath of the Armada campaign brought jubilation to the English side and defeat and despair to the Spanish. The English Admiral, Lord Howard of Effingham, spoke of the 'Invincible Armada' with heavy irony. The Dutch were unable to contain their delight, and cast a series of triumphalist silver medals to commemorate the great defeat. One side of the medal showed the Spanish fleet

Triumphalist silver medal minted by the Dutch after the defeat of the Armada, showing the Spanish fleet dispersed and wrecked. In the clouds above is the name of Jehovah, in Hebrew, and around the edge the famous Latin inscription: *Flavit et dissipati sunt* – He blew and they were scattered.

dispersed and wrecked. In the clouds above is the name of Jehovah in Hebrew. Around the edge is a Latin inscription: *Flavit et dissipati sunt 1588* – He blew and they were scattered.

Philip was shattered by the defeat. He felt God had deserted him and he feverishly looked around for those to blame. Neither the Duke of Parma nor Medina Sidonia were considered culpable, so his wrath fell on Diego Flores de Valdes, Medina Sidonia's chief naval adviser. When the defeated and depleted fleet returned home to Spain, de Valdes was held responsible for the unprecedented disaster. Among the charges against him were that he had persuaded Medina Sidonia to abandon the stricken ship of his cousin – Don Pedro de Valdes – the *Nuestra Senora de la Rosario,* and had left him to become a prisoner of war. Further, he had ordered all the ships' cables to be cut at Calais when the English sent in the fireships, causing them to lose their fighting crescent formation. After evidence had been amassed against him, Philip ordered de Valdes's arrest and sent him to prison in Burgos, northern Spain, where he remained for over a year.

His cousin, Don Pedro, enjoyed greater good fortune. He was a prisoner of war in England, residing in the house of Sir Francis Drake's relatives until 1593. At that time, he was ransomed for 1,500 ducats and returned to Spain. During his sojourn in England he worked on a Spanish-English dictionary, which was published in 1591. Philip continued to think highly of him, and from 1602 until 1608 he held the post of governor of Cuba.

Another high-born prisoner of war who prospered after the defeat was Don Diego Pimentel. He had been commander of the Portuguese galleon the *San Marcos,* which had been driven ashore near Ostend. He was ransomed for the sum of 1,650 ducats and subsequently became viceroy of Mexico in 1624.

The Spanish had suffered greatly. On 3 September 1588, Medina Sidonia wrote to Philip:

> I pray God in his mercy will grant us fine weather so that the Armada may soon enter port; for we are so short of provisions that if for our sins we be long delayed, all will be irretrievably lost. There are now a great number of sick and many die.

The English suffered horribly too. On 20 August 1588, Lord Howard wrote to Sir William Cecil, Lord Burghley, Elizabeth's chief minister of State:

> Sickness and mortality begins wonderfully to grow amongst us; and it is a most pitiful sight to see, here at Margate, how the men, having no place to receive them here, die in the streets. I am driven myself, of force, to come a-land, to see them bestowed in some lodging; and the best I can get is barns and such out-houses.

In reality, the Armada of 1588 did not alter the face of Europe. The victor, England, was left impoverished by the cost of the conflict. The Dutch still required support against the Spanish; the war between Spain and Holland did not end until 1648. Elizabeth again found herself supporting the Huguenot Henri of Navarre against the French Catholics of the Holy League. She was forced to encourage her best seamen to go on piratical adventures in the hopes of filling her coffers again with Spain's wealth. Both Sir John Hawkins and Sir Francis Drake, her best and most experienced naval leaders, perished in 1595 and 1596 respectively in the Spanish Main, when they were attempting a final great assault on wealthy Spanish colonies.

The Irish still had to be kept in a state of subjection in case another Armada could be gathered together; the conquest of Ireland had to be continued until the bitter end. The Battle of Kinsale on 24 December 1601 saw the defeat of the forces under Hugh O'Neill and the final destruction of the Irish lordships. Elizabeth's forces pushed into central Ulster. O'Neill surrendered in 1603, not realising that the Queen had just died. The Flight of the Earls in 1607 saw the exile of O'Neill of Tyrone, O'Donnell of Tyrconnel and Maguire of Fermanagh and some of their followers, who left Ireland for Spain. Their lands were subsequently confiscated by the English to make way for the plantation of Ulster.

The ailing Philip started to build a real royal navy and attempted to gain control of the waters off the Flemish coast. He fortified his bases in the Caribbean and had a series of fast, heavily armed ships constructed to transport the treasure home from the Spanish colonies. He did not give up the idea of another invasion of England, and began to gather together ships and equipment for a second great Armada – an incredible act for a sixty-nine-year-old man who had witnessed the failure and loss of his first 'invincible' enterprise. When news of this defiance reached Elizabeth, she sent a fleet to attack the Spanish fleet as it returned from the West Indies. The English surprised them in Cadiz harbour in June 1596, and after a brief battle they captured the town and set it on fire. The loss of the Indian fleet and the destruction of Cadiz was a terrible blow to Philip. But this indefatigable old man attempted to gather together a further *two* Armadas, but they too became victims of dreadful weather in the Atlantic and were scattered and forced to return home.

Philip II finally died, after a long illness, at the end of July 1598 in his Escorial palace outside Madrid. His reign had seen the greatest flowering of the Spanish Empire, but also the beginnings of its eventual disintegration. Elizabeth died in March 1603, without an heir. Ironically, James VI of Scotland, who was the son of Mary, Queen of Scots, became James I of England. The brilliance and intrigue of Elizabeth's court and the daring of her naval commanders have made the Elizabethan age a memorable one. But it was to be many years before an English navy ruled the waves and Britain began to acquire a great empire of her own.

THE LEGACY OF THE ARMADA

The Ulster Museum has a permanent display of the *Girona* treasures and of artefacts from the two other Armada ships: *La Trinidad Valencera* and *Santa Maria de la Rosa*. The wreck of *La Trinidad Valencera* was recovered in the waters of the Irish Republic. There were many legal problems to be solved concerning the eventual permanent destination of the excavated finds. The Ulster Museum undertook the enormous task of conserving the artefacts. After protracted negotiations between the Ulster Museum, the City of Derry Sub-Aqua Club and the Irish government, it was agreed that the artefacts would be acquired by the Ulster Museum on the condition that it would lend *Trinidad* objects to Derry when a museum was built there. The Tower Museum in Derry has now been open since 1992, and plans have been drawn up to mount a grand display of *Trinidad* finds from the Ulster Museum's collection.

Some of the items on display in the Armada room at the Ulster Museum.

The Spanish Armada has an important place in the history of Ireland. In 1993, the Ulster Museum bought a jewelled pendant. It was an enamelled gold earring of the Madonna and Child, which had been placed in a later gold setting and embellished with an octagonal amethyst and four emeralds at the back (*see* colour section). The Madonna and Child was bordered by an inscription, *The first gift to Mary,* which refers to the sixteenth-century ancestress of the previous owner of the jewel whose family came from Eggington Hall in Derbyshire. Around the gold border was the inscription:

> *When Spanneshe fleet fled home for feare*
> *This golden picktur ther was found*
> *Fast Fixed unto Spanniards eare*
> *Whoo drowned laye on Irish ground Anno 1558*

We do not know who the unidentified Spaniard was or from which shipwreck he came, but he must have been a nobleman to own such a beautiful earring.

The acquisition of the entire *Girona* collection by the Ulster Museum in 1972 was the first time that an entire assemblage from an underwater excavation was purchased by a single institution and preserved for the nation. Much credit must go to the director of the museum at that time, Wilfred A. Seaby, and to the great effort and imagination of the Keeper of Antiquities, Laurence N.W. Flanagan, who recognised the true worth of the find and the potential of maritime archaeology. Credit too must be given to the Northern Ireland government, which provided eighty-five percent of the finance required for the acquisition. The remaining £50,000 had to be raised by public subscription. The sum was raised in six months by people from all walks of life, so great was their generosity and interest in the remarkable find. This public interest has continued at a high level ever since.

Some thirty years after the original finding and excavation of the *Girona*, the site still continues to provide surprises. Because of its importance, in 1993 it became the first protected wreck-site in the north of Ireland. In 1997 a diver was licensed to survey the site and recover any loose archaeological material that might be exposed on the shifting north coast seabed. In 1998 the licensed diver found the twelfth lapis lazuli cameo – it was in excellent condition despite 411 years in the North Sea. Robert Sténuit had found the other eleven and had been sure that there should have been a twelfth, and he was absolutely right.

Such was the overwhelming interest in the find that the Receiver of Wreck, Maritime and Coastguard Agency, allowed the Ulster Museum to display it, with their permission, until the purchase price had been agreed by independent valuation. The agreed price was £35,000 and the museum approached the National Art Collections Fund for assistance with the purchase; the museum was unable to meet the cost itself because of funding freezes. With great generosity, the National Art Collections Fund made the rare decision to purchase it outright for the museum because of the unique circumstances of the find. The twelfth cameo has now rejoined the other eleven, permanently.

The Armada collection has been on public display in the Ulster Museum since 1972. It is the fascinating mix of wealth, personal effects, historical information and the tragedy of a great enterprise doomed that has made the Armada story a magnet for an audience both at home and abroad. In Forthill cemetery, County Galway, there is a grave commemorating some of the Spaniards who perished on Ireland's shores. The Armada's recovered treasures are a memorial to those times of historic conflict and to the players in this grand, tragic, unparalleled drama.

BIBLIOGRAPHY

Connolly, S.J. (ed.). *Oxford Companion to Irish History*. Oxford: Oxford University Press, 1999.

Curtis, E. *A History of Ireland*. London: Methuen & Co. Ltd, 1961.

De Aramburu, M. In *La Armada Invencible I–II*, C.F. Duro. Madrid: 1884–1885.

De Courcy Ireland, J. *Ireland and the Irish in Maritime History*. Ireland: Glendale Press, 1986.

De Cuellar, Captain Francisco. *A letter to His Majesty King Philip II recounting his misadventures in Ireland and elsewhere after the wreck of his ship*. Translated by Henry Dwight Sedgwick Jr. New York: Richmond & Co. Ltd, 1895.

Fallon, N. *The Armada in Ireland*. London: Stanford Maritime Ltd, 1978.

Flanagan, L.N.W. *Ireland's Armada Legacy*. Dublin: Gill and Macmillan, 1988.

Flanagan, L.N.W. 'The oldest extant post-medieval table-fork'. In *Irish Antiquities: Essays in memory of Joseph Raftery*, M. Ryan (ed.). Wicklow: Wordwell, 1998.

Glover, W. 'The Spanish Armada Wrecks of Ireland'. In *Excavating Ships of War*, M. Bound (ed.). International Maritime Archaeology Series, Vol. 2. Shropshire: Anthony Nelson, 1998.

Grieve, Mrs M. *A Modern Herbal: the medicinal, culinary, cosmetic and economic properties, cultivation and folk-lore of herbs, grasses, fungi, etc, Vols I and II*. Connecticut: Hafner Publishing Company, 1970.

Martin, C. and Parker, G. *The Spanish Armada*. London: Thames and Hudson, 1988.

Martin, C. 'La Trinidad Valencera'. In the International Journal of Nautical Archaeology, Vol. 8, 1, 13–38, 1979.

O'Danachair, C. 'Armada Losses on the Irish Coast'. In *The Irish Sword II* (9): 321–331, 1954–1956.

Padfield, P. *Armada*. London: Victor Gollanz, 1988.

Rodger, N.A.M. *The Armada in the Public Records*. London: HMSO, 1988.

Rodriguez-Salgado, M.J. *Armada 1588–1988: The official catalogue of an international Exhibition to commemorate the Spanish Armada*. Britain: Penguin Books in association with the National Maritime Museum of Britain, 1988.

Scandurra, E. 'The Maritime Republics: Medieval and Renaissance ships in Italy'. In A History of Seafaring, G.F. Bass (ed.). London: Thames and Hudson, 1972.

Smith, A.R. (ed.). *Spanish Armada List, 1588*. London: 1886.

Sténuit, Robert. *Treasures of the Armada*. London: Thames and Hudson, 1972.

Wignall, S. *The Spanish Armada Salvage Expedition (1968): A progress report on seven years' research and underwater investigation into the sinking of the Santa Maria de la Rosa*. (Privately circulated)

Exploring the Book of Kells
George Otto Simms

A beautiful and simple introduction to the Book of Kells, one of Ireland's greatest national treasures. George Otto Simms, a world-renowned authority on the Book of Kells, reveals the mysteries hidden in this magnificent manuscript. He introduces the monks who made the book and guides the reader through the intricate detail of this ancient and exotic book.

Hardback £7.99/$11.95/€10.15

Exploring Newgrange
Liam Mac Uistin

This book explores the creation, building and discovery of Newgrange. Why did our Stone Age ancestors spend years building this monument? How did they move huge boulders miles across hilly country and erect them at the site, without the aid of machinery? What do the many symbols inscribed on these stones mean? Here the extent, and limitations, of our knowledge are uncovered in words, illustrations and photographs.

Hardback £7.99/$14.95/€10.15

Exploring Irish Music and Dance
Dianna Boullier

Here for the first time is a book specially for the many people across the world who love Irish music. It gives the background to the music, fascinating information about the instruments, details about tunes, famous events, musicians, different styles and stories about tunes and players. A great source of quirky details and useful basic information. Includes photographs and illustrations

Hardback £7.99/$12.95/€10.15

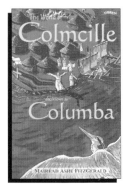

Exploring the World of Colmcille
Mairéad Ashe FitzGerald

A beautifully simple and accessible account of the world of Colmcille/Columba, whose 1,400th anniversary was celebrated in 1997. It deals with the life and times of the saint and his involvement in politics and religious affairs. A man of adventure and charisma from the warrior-aristocracy of Ireland, Colmcille's legacy lives on in legend and history. Draws on the history, art, literature and archaeology of the time.

Paperback £4.99/$11.95/€6.34

The Vikings in Ireland
Morgan Llywelyn

In Irish history the Vikings are often seen merely as invaders. Morgan Llywelyn gives a fascinating account of the wider picture – how the Vikings significantly influenced Irish art and trade and the growth of towns and cities. Cameos of the lives of individual Vikings, some real, some fictitious, bring a liveliness and freshness to the retelling of events which only an author of historical fiction can achieve. Authentic drawings as well as photographs of excavations and artefacts support the text.

Hardback £7.99/$12.95/€10.15

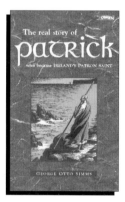

The Real Story of St Patrick
George Otto Simms/Illus. David Rooney

Many legends and stories have grown up over the centuries about Ireland's patron saint. George Otto Simms goes back to Patrick's *Confession* and his other writings to separate the man from the myth. What emerges is a fascinating account of a man of great strength, told in a way that will appeal to both young and old. David Rooney's charming illustrations accompany the text, along with Early Celtic artefacts and details from the ninth-century Book of Armagh.

Paperback £5.50/$7.95/€6.98

Brendan the Navigator

George Otto Simms/Illus. David Rooney

A retelling of Brendan's famous account of his voyages and the extraordinary imagery and unusual events of this ancient story, which was known all over the world in the Middle Ages. Volcanoes, icebergs, sea-monsters, strange beings – all these play a part in this ancient adventure story. Simms unravels the mysteries and wonders of Brendan's travels and explains why and how the voyage was undertaken.

Paperback £4.99/$7.95/€5.71

Celtic Way of Life

Curriculum Development Unit/
Illus. Josip Lizatovic

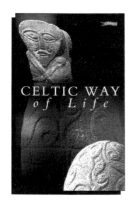

A colourful and warlike people, constantly on the move, the Celts spread from Central Europe to Ireland, bringing with them their beliefs and customs, new crafts and skills, tools and weapons of iron and a Celtic language. Here we explore their home life, work, political structures, rituals, food-gathering and leisure. This book has been an invaluable guide for tourists and natives alike over the last ten years. Illustrated with photographs of Celtic artefacts, maps and superb reconstruction drawings of Celtic life.

Paperback £5.99/$9.95/€7.61

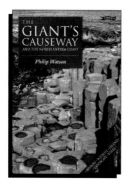